D1106611

This Is How We Dance Now!

This Is How We Dance Now!

*Performance in the Age of Bollywood
and Reality Shows*

PALLABI CHAKRAVORTY

OXFORD

UNIVERSITY PRESS

OXFORD
UNIVERSITY PRESS

Oxford University Press is a department of the University of Oxford.
It furthers the University's objective of excellence in research, scholarship,
and education by publishing worldwide. Oxford is a registered trademark of
Oxford University Press in the UK and in certain other countries.

Published in India by
Oxford University Press
2/11 Ground Floor, Ansari Road, Daryaganj, New Delhi 110 002, India

ISBN-13: 978-0-19-947776-0
ISBN-10: 0-19-947776-0

Typeset in Dante MT Std 10.5/16
by The Graphics Solution, New Delhi 110 092
Printed in India by Rakmo Press, New Delhi 110 020

To the teachers and students of Courtyard Dancers
in Subhasgram (Kolkata) and Philadelphia

Contents

Figures

Acknowledgements

Wth began as simple curiosity about the backup dancers in Bombay/Bollywood films developed into this persistent and in-depth study of dance reality shows, the new remixed dances, their dancers and choreographers in urban India. This book has been a journey of manifolds; there are many individuals and institutions that made it possible.

I begin with the institution where I have been teaching for the past 16 years, Swarthmore College, Pennsylvania, USA. I was supported with the Brand Blanshard award from Swarthmore, two small research grants, and two sabbatical leaves between 2011–12 and 2015–16 to research and write this manuscript. The manuscript grew and changed shape with the help of comments by individuals at conferences and presentations in various academic institutions such as Jadavpur University, Kolkata, University of Chicago, US, Kyoto University, Japan,University of California, US, Santa Barbara, Texas A&M University, US, City University of New York, US, the Dance History Scholars Association (SDHS) conference in Philadelphia, the South Asia conference in Madison, the International Federation for Theater Research (IFTR) conference in Hyderabad, India, and a Dance Studies colloquium at Temple University, US. My heartfelt thanks to all these individuals who are too numerous to name here.

I would especially like to thank media scholar Nilanjana Gupta for her detailed and critical comments on this manuscript. In addition, I extend my thanks to Moinak Biswas, Kaley Mason, Douglas Rosenberg, Sherill Dodds, Pika Ghosh, Gayatri Chatterji, Abhijit Roy, Aishika Chakraborty, Priya Srinivasan, and Urmimala Sarkar for their enthusiasm and support for this project. I am grateful to Bollywood choreographers Geeta Kapoor, Jay Borade, Vikram Borade, Begum Habiba, and art director Sanjay Dabade, and film director John Matthew for their generosity of time. I would also take this opportunity to thank my childhood friends Baisakhi Ghosh, who connected me to the film industry in Mumbai, and Priyadarshini Ghosh, for her contacts among reality show dancers in Kolkata. The dancers and choreographers in Kolkata; Sanjukta Ray, Bhaskar Raut, and Sajid Jamal were central to this project and I will be forever grateful to them for their spirit, courage, and generosity. There are many unnamed dancers and choreographers, set builders, tea delivery boys, auto drivers, mothers, and teachers who contributed to this project and I extend my deep gratitude to them. I would also like to thank the National Film Archive of India (NFAI) in Pune for letting me include the photographs in this book, and the Film Studies Department in Jadavpur University, Kolkata, for allowing me to use their archives and libraries. To Donna Fournier in the Underhill library at Swarthmore College, my abiding gratitude for finding me books and articles and to Andrew Hauze, my colleague at Swarthmore, a heartfelt thanks for his input on the western musical influences on Bollywood songs.

This book simply would not have its current shape without the incisive editing skills and critical comments by my husband, who is the sounding board for all my projects; intellectual and creative. Incidentally, he is one of the best writers I know. I am thankful for such lucky accidents of life! Our son, who is now studying in Australia, and is following a passion that is his very own. I am grateful to have such a family of diverse passions and convictions that makes my own journeys, such as this, both pleasurable and possible.

Lens on Reality

I set out to meet Allen sir (as he was popularly known) one afternoon with Chandan, the driver of my rented car. Chandan was my human GPS (Global Positioning System) who could take me anywhere. But we did not have proper directions to Allen sir's house, which was located in some dense and deep alleyways of south Kolkata, well beyond the movie studios in Tollygunge. We knew the name of the church next to his house and we stopped our car at different junctures to ask for directions. Everybody we asked, from auto drivers to pedestrians to shopkeepers, knew the directions to Allen sir's house. They all knew him from TV. Chandan was pleased that I was meeting someone famous and important; he asked whether we were going to a politician's or a film star's house.

Allen Perris, the choreographer of the reality show *Dance Bangla Dance (Junior),* was neither a politician nor a film star, but a young Christian male from a modest background who became a household name in Kolkata in 2011. Not only was he a household name, but his name evoked strong sentiments for dance, culture, and reality shows among and children and adults alike. He became synonymous with a constellation of images regularly seen on Bangla television which kept the audiences hooked. It was evident from the sentiments expressed by many people I spoke with, that dance reality shows were unsettling the taken-for-granted cultural domain of Indian dance and music. It was a very visible part of India's emergent but unwieldy public culture that was drawing a huge diversity of agents into its folds, both as participants and spectators. The stage was new, uncharted, and tantalizing. The audiences were passionate and captivated.

I found Allen Perris in his tiny flat with a bandana around his head and a loose fitting T-shirt. He was soft spoken, modest, and accessible. He was excited about his future as a choreographer of reality shows. Currently working for Zee TV, he was looking forward to work with Star TV and other networks. He said that the audience had high standards now and it wanted novelty—although authenticity was good, it had to be blended, like Bharatanatyam with Contemporary dance. The last episode of *Dance Bangla Dance* he told me, had a multitude of dance categories such as Latin, Creative, Contemporary Indian, Hip-Hop, and Bollywood. He had won the best choreographer's award, despite the presence of other wonderful choreographers on the show, who blended international dance styles, acrobatics, and Bollywood to create new forms and choreographies—something I call 'remix'.[1]

This was the new dance landscape that was revolutionizing the established Indian dance hierarchies of classical, folk, tribal, and filmy. These rigid categories of Indian dances (created by the past elite nationalist narratives and by the state akademies in Delhi) were dissolving in contemporary India. A cultural war was taking place, far away from the strident corridors of party politics, and it was ushering in a new vision of a participatory democracy. A new generation of dancers and choreographers was emerging, many of them were from the lower

---

[1] The 'remix' style is different than what is known as modern Indian dance that was ushered in by Uday Shankar and Tagore. Their ideologies and the class formations were also very different than what shapes 'remix' (see Purkayastha [2014] for a discussion on the dance styles of Tagore and Shankar).

middle and working classes with diverse caste and religious identities, as cultural producers and consumers. Indian democracy was spreading wider and digging deeper, and the older classical dances were losing their hold as the sources of symbolic capital for status and identity. These dramatic transformations in cultural values and their meanings accompanied India's economic liberalization. That structural shift had ushered in the rise and spread of Bollywood as a culture industry, along with an astounding explosion of television channels. This multiplication of cable and satellite channels rapidly changed India's public sphere into a chaotic morass. It spawned a transnational and translocal cultural ethos that contested the erstwhile bounded national and regional (and gender) identities. The debates on market reforms continued to rage in many quarters, and as the Narendra Modi government came to power in 2014, with the promise of further reforms and economic development, but also with the ideology of Hindu right-wing politics, the debates on morality and good conduct intensified even further.

These rapid and tumultuous changes of the past two decades could be seen as a bewildering ensemble of contradictions. The core contradiction was between a globalizing economy and culture advocating a Janus-faced narrative of modernization, urbanization, and democratization on one side, and a counter-narrative of preservation of tradition, sacred places, and the environment from laissez-faire development and westernization on the other side. These competing narratives played out at different scales, from being entrenched in the micro-politics of the local and the vernacular to that of the national. The momentum of change facilitated various kinds of boundary-crossings among cultural forms such as between 'high' and 'low', classical and folk, Indian and western, consequently breaking down received and accepted classifications. The most important aspect of this chaotic newness was the spread of media, electronic communication, and globalization. The articulations and practices of Indian dance took center stage in the mushrooming of visual culture circulated by new media and technology. One such new cultural form is the dance reality shows on TV. These Bollywood-inspired remixed global dances are arguably the most visible cultural product of India's new economy (other than Bollywood film itself).

This book composes a multi-layered theoretical paradigm to locate, historicize, and analyse the dances in dance reality shows as both an aesthetic cultural product and the lived reality of a new generation of dancers and choreographers who are among the emergent 'aspirational Indians' in the new global economy. Drawing on ethnographic fieldwork in Kolkata and Mumbai (2006–12) and archival research at the National Film Institute, Pune, this book explores the emergence of 'remixed' styles such as Bollywood dances (derived from the song and dance sequences of Bombay / Bollywood films) and dance reality shows in shaping the contours and ambivalences of India's new public culture along with new identities of femininity and masculinity.[2]

Dance Anthropology in a New Terrain

This multi-sited ethnographic project is an attempt to use the lens of dance and dancers to make sense of some of the profound changes

---

[2] The new dimensions of public culture (with India as the focus) were discussed in the book *Consuming Modernity* by Appadurai and Breckenridge (1995) and were also debated on the pages of the journal *Public Culture*. It was further theorized in the book *Modernity at Large* by Appadurai (1997). I will not reiterate the debates here. However, I will emphasize that in many ways they break from and complicate the Habermasian notion of the 'public sphere' and expand its scope in terms of 'global flows' and 'scapes' to articulate the cultural dimensions of globalization. Interestingly, the question of 'flow' has also been central to televisual reception as espoused by Raymond Williams (1974). Its potential to shed light on the contemporary Indian television culture through a reworking of the notion of 'flow' has been discussed by Roy (2014).

taking place in Indian culture today. I follow in the footsteps of many anthropologists and propose to unpack some of the most fundamental issues in cultural change in India by looking closely at one of its most visible and cosmopolitan yet local manifestations, the dance reality show. In the process, I show, from the vantage point of an ethnographic eye, how a particular kind of consumerist modernity is performed in contemporary India.

The crisis of representation in the 1980s was a watershed in the discipline of anthropology.[3] It facilitated the emergence of new domains of inquiry under the rubric of 'public culture' (Appadurai and Breckenridge 1995; Mazzarella 2004). Interestingly, these theoretical and methodological recalibrations in anthropology paralleled the economic reforms in India which formally began in 1991. My voice as an ethnographer and the voices of the subjects of the research represented here were all caught up in this vortex of change that was unravelling the past codes of 'cultural authenticity' (associated with a constructed narrative of cultural essence and brahminical tradition—both of which are ingrained in the discourses of classical Indian dance, cultural authority, and elite power). As a Kathak dance artist myself, trained in the tradition of the *gurukul* system (belonging to the lineage of a guru), I had to constantly be vigilant about my own assumptions and tastes about culture, aesthetics, meaning, and tradition. The globalization of culture and economy in India was remapping tastes and 'cultural distinctions' at an unprecedented rate, and I, along with the subjects of this research, was bewildered, restless, and looking for clarity (Bourdieu 1984). I was often self-conscious about my own interest in dance reality shows because the hierarchical classical-contemporary dance world I normally

---

[3] The 'crisis of representation' that raged in the 1980s (Clifford and Marcus 1986; Marcus and Fisher 1986; Fox 1991) had its roots in visual anthropology, especially the anthropology of visual representation (see Hymes 1962; Worth 1976; Ruby 1980).

inhabit as a practitioner, which is often positioned in binary terms, did not view commercial forms such as these as 'art' and thus deemed them unworthy of academic or artistic scrutiny. The dancers and choreographers of the reality shows I was interacting with were all too aware of the criticisms and controversies directed at them and were self-reflexive about their own engagement with reality shows.

As an anthropologist of Indian dance and culture and a performing artist myself, questions of representation, ethics, and power relations in both the worlds of art and fieldwork were especially troubling at multiple levels. Globalization did not make the world flat; it highlighted the deep inequalities within and between the cultures and groups that anthropologists study, throwing into relief the inadequacies of the simple binaries of cultural insiders and outsiders. Interestingly, my identity as a cultural insider did not create any easy rapport with the communities of dancers and choreographers I interacted with during my fieldwork. To that community, I was an outsider. Not because I was based in the US but because I was identified as a classical dancer, a cultural identity that made me a 'purist' rather than a fellow dancer in some of their eyes.[4] For instance, the famous Bollywood choreographer Saroj Khan refused to talk to me in Mumbai after hearing of my background as a Kathak dancer, claiming that her dancing and her choreographies were antithetical to the classical arts.[5]

In addition, the continuous adjustments of meeting schedules and the unpredictable work habits and mobile lifestyles of the choreographers

---

[4] The discourses of purity regarding the classical arts are an aspect of the selective appropriation of the traditional dance practices in India during Indian nationalism, and is still perpetuated by many revered gurus and their students. It is a theme that recurs at several points in this book.

[5] It is to be noted, however, that Saroj Khan herself was trained in Kathak by her husband and Bombay film choreographer B. Sohanlal.

created a challenge, at times, to plan a fieldwork strategy. However, once I got accustomed to the uncertainties, I had deep and lasting interactions with many individual dancers and choreographers. Many of them generously shared their time and insights and allowed me to observe their classes and their artistic work with enthusiasm and kindness. I was even invited to dance in Bollywood choreographer Begum Habiba's studio in Mumbai with her students (Figure 1.1). This novel experience made me aware of my inadequacies to move like a Bollywood dancer. It also made me acutely aware of the embodied nature of ethnographic fieldwork, which was not just about my expertise in dance, but my abilities to engage the senses. The investigation of the sensory dimensions of the dance reality shows was integral to my own embodied experiences during the fieldwork. My awkwardness and enjoyment in many ethnographic moments reflected my negotiations of class, gender, bodily habituations, and their mediations.

FIGURE 1.1   Begum Habiba's Class, Mumbai
Source: Author.

Thus, 'embodiment and experience' emerged as important analytical concepts as they intersected with media and technology in my analysis of dance reality shows. This book is an exploration of the sentiments and intimacies as well as the distances and ambivalences created by the performances and mediations of the dancing body. Economic liberalization and globalization in contemporary India are the large structural forces that are driving change, no doubt, but the change is felt not merely through the tangible and the visible, but also through minute, personal and intimate senses, in short, in the sensorium of the hidden perceptions of non-verbal communications.

The social implications of the visual media and the sensory dimensions of our engagement with them have been central to the debates on media and culture from Marshall McLuhan to the Frankfurt school (Mazzarella 2004). The globalization and mediation of culture have deeply inflected the questions surrounding cultural authenticity and authority, which have destabilized notions of the 'real'. These questions have not only unsettled past categories of high and low culture but have complicated the certainties of our social experience through the mediation of the virtual and the actual. Now, experience itself is the interplay of different media. This in turn has complicated the notions of nearness and distance, the temporal and scalar dimensions of the 'real' (Mazzarella 2004). Dance reality shows (and reality shows in general) exemplify these profound ambivalences of contemporary Indian culture where past categories and experiences are in dynamic flux causing the 'real' and the 'authentic' to blur endlessly. Mazzarella (2004: 356) writes:

> As anthropologists of media and globalization, we confront a world in which cynicism about social functions of the media and romanticism about authenticity and value of culture are equally widespread. These two phenomena are, moreover, related, and their interrelationship arises, in part, out of the profound ambivalence that a heightened self-consciousness about the mediated quality of our lives has produced.

This especially creates an intensely paradoxical experience when we juxtapose the embodiment of dance with media. The intersections of modern entertainment media—cinema, television, and music videos—with older traditions of ritual, music, dance, and theatre are complex areas of investigation where several overlapping spheres of meaning, senses, emotions, and contestations are simultaneously at play. In the modern age of mechanical reproduction, the visual aesthetics of the past (derived from Indian philosophical, religious, and secular traditions) entangle with modern technologies of imaging from photography to YouTube videos. Using an interrelated but discrete theoretical collage from anthropology, performance studies, film and media studies, and Indian aesthetic theories, this book launches an exploration of this rich history and variety of the performance-visual continuum as it interfaces with the media explosion of screen dance. It is necessary to dig deep into theory in order to understand how these inter-media interaction shapes the diverse tapestry of lives, desires, aspirations, and experiences of dancers and choreographers in contemporary India.

The important themes I explore are subjectivity, media-embodiment, pedagogy, gender identity, and social mobility, and the specific questions I address are:

- How do desire and emotion/affect intersect with new media in shaping contemporary subjectivities?
- What is the relationship between Bombay/Bollywood film dance and the remixed dances shown on reality shows?
- How do pedagogical shifts in learning to dance from gurukul systems to more recent varied urban settings change the experiences of embodiment? How does the production of song and dance sequences in Bollywood films and TV reality shows influence these pedagogical and aesthetic shifts?

- How are individual subjectivities forged by aspirational desires expressed through dancing and everyday life experiences? Do such aspirations create alternative spaces for participation in cultural processes, enumeration of democracy, and citizenship?
- Why do the 'remix' dances in reality shows open up debates on morality, femininity and masculinity, cultural authenticity, modernity, and middle-class respectability?

The various chapters in this book are my attempts to answer these questions. My search for meaning and explanation involved several years of ethnographic fieldwork, archival research, and content analysis of reality shows on TV and YouTube.

My ethnographic fieldwork among reality show dancers and choreographers took place at three different sites: Film City Studios in Mumbai, dance classes in Mumbai and Kolkata, and reality TV auditions in Kolkata. These sites also highlight the overlapping worlds of Bollywood and dance reality shows and the ongoing construction of the new 'remix' aesthetics and (what I identify as) the 'copy and paste' media-embodiment. For instance, through immersive participant observation in film studios, dance studios, and dance classes in Mumbai and Kolkata, I show how methods of transmission of bodily knowledge (even within the commercial settings of commodity production) lead to improvisation and artistic creativity. This, in turn, enables the marginal choreographers of reality shows to become cultural entrepreneurs and agents. Later I show that this intersection of everyday dance practice and its 'habitus' among reality show dancers expands the notion of 'habitus' as not just an arena of cultural reproduction, but of change and dynamism (Bourdieu 1977; Born 2010).

If the artistic, creative, and pedagogic aspects of these dances were visible in the studios, classes, rehearsals, and performances, the lives of the dancers and choreographers had to be found elsewhere—inside their homes, listening to them and their family members, or in private conversations that took place away from home and work. I locate human agency within the quotidian lives of the reality show dancers and choreographers through in-depth semi-structured and open-ended interviews and personal life histories of selected individuals. At one level, the structural transformations underway in India have to be understood through the frameworks of globalization, mediation, and the market; but at another level, in some ways a more meaningful one, the explorations and explanations of agency have to be situated in the ethnographic local and the mundane 'every day'.

These ethnographic experiences are deepened with archival research in Pune's National Film Institute and the Department Film Studies at Jadavpur University, Kolkata. The archival work enables me to construct a sensory and visual history of screen dances. Although this is a selective history of song and dance sequences in Bombay/Bollywood films, it provides a critical narrative link to the development of visual and media culture in India through the lens of the dancing body. The visual and content analysis of reality shows on national and local TV in India and on YouTube further propel my examination of the aesthetic transformations of 'rasa' to 'remix'.

The Following Chapters

Chapter 2, titled 'Ways of Seeing', broadly situates human subjectivity, desire, and senses/emotions in a large literature in which desire and the desiring subject are central to discourses on aesthetics and identity. The epistemological excursions I undertake in this chapter are necessary to provide a context for my exploration of aesthetic shifts and embodiment as they connect to human subjectivity, agency, and affect in contemporary media culture.[6] This chapter is divided into three sections:

---

[6] I use the terms 'affect' and 'emotion' here without underlining their specific meanings and discursive configurations (see Mazzarella 2009).

'Unpacking Desire from Continental Philosophy to Media Theory'; 'Anthropological Interventions and the Universal Subject of Desire'; and 'Indian Philosophy, Embodied Aesthetics, Filmic Desire'. I draw on discourses of desire spanning continental philosophy to psychoanalytical theory to Indian aesthetic theory to film and media theory. The construction of desire through the chapter 'Ways of Seeing' remains central to the formation of subjectivity, whether it is informed by a Marxian notion of 'aura' of the commodity form, Walter Benjamin's aura as 'authenticity,' 'fetish' in psychoanalytical theory, or 'gaze' in the Indian idea of 'darshan' or 'nazar' (Berger 1972; Haug 1986; Shaviro 1993; Stratton 1996; Vasudevan 2000; Bhatti and Pinney 2011). Hence, analysing the discursive formation of desire across various disciplinary boundaries allows me to locate the deep perceptual and aesthetic shifts underway in India as crystallized through the dance reality shows.

Moreover, the focus on identity formation through the framework of desire underlines the theoretical intersections and limitations of film and media theories in analysing screen dances from a cross-cultural perspective. However, I also show that the sensory dimensions of dance and the screen can open up new experiences of affect/emotion and such dimensions are exciting new ground for cultural inquires (Kavka 2008; Kumar 2006). I propose that the analysis of affect/emotion and desire through Indian aesthetics expressed in dance and films adds a new texture to the usual understanding of the cinematic image and television spectacle (Kaur and Sinha 2005; Punathambekar and Kavoori 2008; Dudhra and Desai 2008). This theoretical mosaic provides the foundation for my investigation of embodied aesthetics and individual agency in dance reality shows in contemporary India.

Chapter 3 titled 'Screens and Dances', focuses on the intersection of film technology and dance has a long history in India. Rather than analysing the dance reality show as a western import, this chapter traces the origins of these shows to the song and dance choreographies of

Bombay films, which began to be known as Bollywood only from the 1980s. The chapter is divided into three sections. In the first section, 'The Desiring Subject of the Songs and Dances', desire (in the context of film, dance, and Indian aesthetic theory) forms the theoretical lens to explore the song and dance sequences as aspects of both aesthetic and material desire in shaping Indian citizen-subjects. The second section, 'Bombay Filmi Nach to Bollywood Dance', explores the song and dance sequences that negotiate the cross-currents of indigenous aesthetics and western cosmopolitanism to create an enduring tension between tradition and modernity. The third section titled 'Mixing Bhavas to Remix', analyses the fragmentation and emergence of the new aesthetics of 'remix' in Bollywood song and dance sequences. The three sections together establish a genealogical and sensory link between Bombay/Bollywood film dance and television reality shows.

The use of the choreographic form in creating cinematic spectacles integrating staging, costumes, sets, lighting, and camera angles was associated with the film medium from its inception. I use some key song and dance sequences from past Bombay films and contemporary Bollywood—in films ranging from *Kalpana, Inder Sabha, Alam Ara, Chandralekha, Shakuntala, Rajnartaki, Jhanak Jhanak Payal Baje, Diamond Queen, Howrah Bridge, Mughal-E-Azam, Guide, Pakeezah, Umrao Jaan, Hum Kissi Se Kum Nahin, Disco Dancer, Tezaab, Khalnayak, Dil Se, Hum Apke Hain Kaun, Dhoom 2,* and *Tees Mar Khan*—to show the journey of dance from Hindi films to dance reality shows. In delineating this pathway, I show, in particular, how 'item numbers' in Bollywood have evolved from the traditional '*mujras*'. There is a long history of relationships between Bombay films, the video industry, and television in constructing the screen history and cultural identity of Indian dances. This chapter details that modernizing tradition.

Chapter 4 which is titled 'Flexing and Remixing Bodies' focuses on 'remix' dances as they are choreographed and performed in film studios (such as Mumbai's Film City) and television reality show auditions (such as *Dance India Dance*) as well as in classes and rehearsals. This chapter has three sections. In the first section, 'Embodiment of Devotional Desire to Commodity Desire' I briefly analyse the traditional training system of *gurushisya parampara* that was adopted and adapted by the modern institutions of dance training in India and examine how the contemporary dominance of screen dances is changing the ideology, aesthetics, and contexts of pedagogy. The focus on these pedagogical transitions highlight the aesthetic transitions of embodiment of desire associated with the yogic or transcendental bodies of classical dances to remixed consumerist bodies of reality shows. These transitions also map the changing relationship between 'high' culture and 'popular' culture. The second section, 'Producing a Sequence', is located in Film City in Mumbai. Here, I explore the process of choreography, camera angles, and image-making in constructing the song and dance sequences for Bollywood movies. I also represent the voices of some leading Bollywood choreographers as they reflect on their personal experiences with the commodification of aesthetics from the past codes of mythopoetic constructs. In the third section, 'Dancing between Mumbai and Kolkata', the focus shifts to the actual dance training in the dance halls in Mumbai and dance classes and studios in Kolkata to analyse the pedagogical changes in training the body, especially among the reality show dancers and choreographers. Among the ethnographic sites I cover is an audition of hundreds of hopefuls for the hit reality show, *Dance India Dance*, held in Kolkata in 2012.

Overall, the chapter focuses on 'embodiment' to examine how the dominant aesthetic emotion (*rasa*) derived from mythopoetic concepts of desire and associated with song and dance sequences in films, is transformed not only through technological and aesthetic innovations on screen but through the actual training of the body in dance halls, studios, classes, and rehearsals. The embodiment of 'remix' as the new

aspirational emotion describes the interconnections between new training techniques, film editing, and choreography of new Indian dances.
In order to explore Indian dance in this present condition, the phenomenological concept of 'embodiment' offers us insights into how desires/
aspirations are experienced and moulded through the interactions with
technology and consumerism in contemporary Indian culture.

The three ethnographic settings highlight the overlapping worlds of
Bollywood and dance reality shows and the ongoing construction of
the new 'remix' aesthetics and 'copy and paste' embodiment. The new
aesthetics include mixing and mediation (also remixing and remediation) of Bollywood freestyle dances with western style Hip-Hop, Salsa,
Modern, Contemporary, and traditional Indian dances such as classical
and folk and all sorts of hybrid forms that are in-between. The chapter
also highlights the diverse subject positions of the contestants in reality
shows who come from many backgrounds and social spaces ranging
from the middle to the working classes. The participants do not belong
to the usual hereditary lineages of performing artists, nor are they from
elite backgrounds as is usually the case for classical dancers. For them,
media exposure is their opportunity to be visible and counted among
the cultural participants of India's expanding democracy.

The next chapter is titled 'Mediated Subjectivities'. It alights briefly
on the struggle for private sector autonomy in Indian television before
focusing on the emergence of dance reality shows on national and
regional television networks. It also includes life histories of a few
reality show dancers and choreographers to delve into their personal
struggles, aspirations, and achievements. The purpose is to focus on
the televisual and lived experiences of the dancers and choreographers
and connect the production of spectacles on the screen to their everyday lives. The chapter is divided into three sections. The first section is
'Television History and Autonomy' and it looks at the recent development and massive growth of cable TV networks after a long period of

state control. The second section, 'Remix and Dance Reality Shows', analyses the spread of reality shows through various media networks. It connects the industry of Bollywood to television and other electronic media (to highlight their symbiotic relations) and focuses on two reality shows, one regional and one national, to describe and analyse their contents. The third section, 'Digitized Desires in Everyday Life', builds life histories of a few individual choreographers and dancers of reality shows to connect their everyday experiences and struggles to their dancing on screen. Their life histories illuminate how their subjectivities are shaped through their everyday experiences and embodiments of dancing on and off screen. We hear their perspectives on how reality shows such as *Dhum Machale* and *Just Dance* give them a platform to pursue their dreams of success.

Chapter 6 titled 'A Struggle for Identity', focuses on the transformation of desire through the public debates on westernization, middle-class respectability, and exploitation of women and children that are provoked by dance reality shows. It is important to recognize that these shows open up both public and private battlegrounds in the ongoing transformation of the sensory and material desires connected to consumerism, democracy, and modernity. This reflection on the heated debates surrounding India's transition to a liberalizing nation and its embrace of a consumerist ideology is done in three sections. In the first section, 'Everybody Wants to Be Modern', I analyse the dance reality show as a site not only for class mobility but also the anxieties and promises of a new social order as it engages in the construction of new cultural authorities, new ideals of femininity and masculinity ('item girls' and 'item boys'), and new cosmopolitan Indians. The second section on 'Morality and Corruption' focuses on the discursive debates regarding reality shows, media, and the lure of fame and corruption that continues to trouble middle-class morality. It also reflects on the grave dangers lurking in the right-wing moral rhetoric of cultural pollution associated with the current government in India. The third section, 'Sexual Politics and Dance Desires', looks specifically at ordinary women and their struggles to claim a modern respectable identity through commercial dance platforms such as dance reality shows.

***

This book argues that dance forges a specific experience and raises an important set of debates on India's ongoing encounter with modernity.[7] In order to understand and analyse the present hybridization and spectacularization of culture due to media and globalization, it explores the relationships between dance, body, screen, and consumerist modernity as they entangle with notions of desire. It focuses on the changing aesthetics of Indian dance due to new media, the role of media and dance in the construction of modern subjects, the remixed dance genres and embodiment, the changing gender codes, the rise of popular culture and democracy, and the construction of new cultural authorities and the power of celebrity culture. The rapid and unprecedented changes that liberalization unleashed in India also eroded some of the earlier moral and ethical codes of culture. This book situates Indian dance at the crossroads of such an ethical and aesthetic transformation. In all this momentum of change, locating agency in the ordinary citizen subject remains paramount.

---

[7] This does not mean that modernity is understood here as a singular discourse stemming from a universal Euro-American model but is premised upon a multiple and contested framework (Chakrabarty 2000).

Ways of Seeing

In a lecture titled 'Man the Artist' delivered in 1930, Rabindranath Tagore discussed the evolution of man from the apes to the ideal state of human consciousness; the person possessing this ideal state, according to him, is a 'music maker', in other words, an artist. According to Tagore (1930), creativity is what makes us human. The subjectivity of a creative being thus quintessentially defines humanity for Tagore and he argues for creativity to be understood as a fundamental desire of life itself, simply put, as the desire to exist, 'to be'.

This core or fundamental understanding of desire may be true even today, but desire has a radically different meaning in post-liberalization India. The globalization of culture has promised a new kind of citizenship to Indians, one which is swathed in a sensory world of images, sounds, and commodities fuelled by new media, new practices of consumption, and new desires. These new desires (I propose) can be analysed by focusing on the embodied aesthetic shifts, of which the dancing body is the most visible expression. Since contemporary India is marked by what may be called 'voluptuous-consumerist desire', this chapter will explore the myriad meanings of desire and subjectivity in various scholarly discourses, from the east and the west, in order to analyse its contours and significance for contemporary culture. I look, therefore, at the discursive formation of desire in terms of human consciousness and subjectivity through the lenses of knowledge, reason, power, fetish, gaze, affect, and emotion across many disciplinary boundaries to show its heterogeneous meaning. My argument then converges to show that desire and subjectivity in contemporary India can be best analysed through the lens of aesthetic desire and embodied subjectivities. Therefore, I take 'desire' as the key concept not only for looking at the aesthetic shifts in Indian dance but for the larger investigations of human consciousness, subjectivity, and identity-formation in the scholarly traditions in the humanities and social sciences. Although anthropology is my disciplinary anchor and accordingly I am interested in exploring how conceptual frameworks can be connected to our lived experiences and are not merely abstractions, I begin from philosophy. The epistemological excursions I indulge in here are necessary to provide a deep context for the subsequent explorations of desire, emotion, and subjectivity in contemporary Indian culture. These explorations are necessary to underline the relevance of sensory perceptions to aesthetic emotion and their connections to mediated realities in shaping modern subjectivities.

The material in this chapter is organized in three sections, each with one or more subsections. I begin with 'Unpacking Desire from Continental Philosophy to Media Theory' (with subsections on Desire, Fetish, Subjectivity; Gaze and Media; and Affect and the Body). The second section is on 'Anthropological Interventions and the Universal Subject of Desire' (with a subsection on Visual Anthropology, Culture, and Emotion) and the third section is on 'Indian Philosophy, Embodied Aesthetics, Filmic Desire' (with subsections on Bodily Knowledge and Self; Indian Performance Theory; and Indian Film Theory and Darshan/ Gaze).

However, the main areas of investigation in this chapter can be further broken into the following intellectual trajectories that deal with the singular question of *desire and subjectivity*:

- Continental philosophy and its intersections with psychoanalytical and media/film theory
- Corporeality and image in the discourses of affect/emotion, aesthetics, desire, and technology, where the body is not just representational (as in film/media theory) but also experiential
- Anthropological interventions in the construction of the Eurocentric universal subject and the debate on culture and experience
- Shifting the focus to Indian classical philosophy, desire, and consciousness, and its conjunction with Indian performance theory and embodied aesthetics
- Indian aesthetic theory and its relevance to films, media, and dance in constructing the citizen-subject

Unpacking Desire from Continental Philosophy to Media Theory

Desire, Fetish, Subjectivity

The desire to know and to create are essential to being human, as Tagore tells us in the quote above (Tagore 1930). Not surprisingly the equation of human consciousness to knowledge and the quest for absolute knowledge have been the fundamental basis of all philosophy, whether eastern or western. However, their approaches have been fundamentally different. In the Renaissance quest for revitalization of knowledge, we find desire and knowledge are wedded together. The desire to know all things—the universe, nature, bodies, and machines—informs the continental thinkers from the seventeenth century onwards. The desire to know also expresses itself as political desire, the will to control others and ultimately to conquer nature. The use of reason to acquire knowledge dominates various fields of human endeavour, as rational thinking and desire are linked together. As desire is disaggregated from passion, we find in this period a conflict between passion and knowledge. Silverman explains (2006: 6):

> If desire is the proper exercise of reason, then significant achievements in self knowledge are possible. But if desire becomes passion—even excessive passion, there is a problem, for often this conflict produces a conflict of choice as well.

If reason and passion are the two opposing aspects of desire that lead to self-knowledge, then the desiring subjects of the romantic period lean towards the latter. In the poetry of Keats and Shelly, feeling and emotion are the expressions of desire and they come from our innermost nature. Here self-knowledge comes from knowing one's emotion rather than reason. The desire for power and control associated with reason, and the desire for feeling or psyche associated with passion, set the stage for the ultimate dichotomy between the formations of 'true' subjectivity. This dialectic emerges with full complexity in Hegelian and Freudian thought. Silverman (2006:8) summarizes:

> This dichotomy between desire and power frames the twentieth century continental tradition. Desire in continental philosophy is either erotic, poetic, loving, transgressive, and insidious or an encounter with the other—productive, creative, and discursive—and expressive of power.

In continental philosophy, the dialectic between desire and power forms the basis of Hegelian thought. The birth of consciousness or to recognize oneself (self-consciousness) through desire is a source of this dialectic. Judith Butler, in her book *Subjects of Desire* (1999: 33; Salih 2002), explains that the German word for desire is both 'animal desire' and 'philosophical desire'. In Hegel's phenomenology, the subject gains knowledge through the recognition and overcoming of difference between self and other. For Hegel, desire is the source for integrating the ontological entity of the subject through the triadic process of thesis, antithesis, and synthesis. However, for Freud, and later for Lacan and Butler, desire prompts the disintegration of the subject rather than create coherence (Salih 2002).

In *Phenomenology of the Spirit* (1807), Hegel explores the relationship between master and slave through the trope of desire and power: the slave desires the position of the master, but the master possesses power over the slave. But this relationship of domination and subordination is not merely about power. It is converted in Hegelian analysis to an achievement of self-consciousness through a relationship between self and other. For Hegel, self-awareness is concomitant to others being conscious of us (that is the master gains his recognition or attains self-knowledge only because the slave desires to be the master; see Silverman 2006). From this productive understanding of desire, it is necessary to consider Freud for whom desire arises from a 'lack' and subjectivity is constituted through sexual drives. Lacan later takes up this idea, but disengages it from the materiality of the body or psychosexual drives to the purely psychic and political realm. But for both Freud and Lacan, subjects are not coherent individuals of Hegelian thought, but fractured by various unconscious drives (Butler 1999).

Thus, desire becomes associated with various prohibitions. It is driven by a castration complex of the male subject. The patriarchal law or taboo against incest adds to it. The prohibition arising out of desire is then linked to the child's entry into the symbolic order of language (Lacan 1949, 2010). In Lacanian psychoanalytical theory, subjectivity and identity formation is integral to language acquisition. We find that Freud, Lacan, and Butler theorize gender, sex, and sexuality within the linguistic or symbolic order and argue that these gendered and sexual identities are generated through the category of the 'desiring subject'. According to Freud, the idea of fetish arising out of the castration complex is an effect of desire and is associated with the male experience. It is dependent on sight (the child realizing the phallic lack in the mother).

Theorists such as Lacan, Mulvey, and others take up this conceptualization of sight as part of identity formation in theorizing the cinematic gaze (Lacan1949/2010; Mulvey 1975). In short, language and sight in convergence with reason and power become key to identity formation and subjectivity in this branch of social theory.

Jon Stratton argues that Freud's preoccupation with fetish and desire speaks to the cultural order of the late nineteenth century in Western capitalist society, which he identifies with the development of sight/gaze as spectacle or 'spectacularization'. Following Thomas Richards, Stratton describes the Great Exhibition of 1851 as a landmark moment for advertising in England. Richards' book *The Commodity Culture of Victorian England* argues for 'the use of the commodity as a semiotics medium—as icon, commemorative, utopia, language, phenomenology, annunciation; in a word, as spectacle' (Stratton 1996: 29). The idea of spectacle is associated with scopophilia (fetishistic gaze) and the commodity form comes to be associated with such desire. In Freud's psychosexual development through the Oedipus complex, the male becomes fetishistic and the female the object of the male fetish, and in a phallocentric world marked as the 'other'. The eroticization of the female body as object and spectacle is then a product of Freudian fetish. This fetish is ultimately projected towards consumption of cultural products where commodity fetishism intersects with cultural fetishism (Stratton 1996). Stratton argues that the spread of cultural fetishism is bound up with the promise of 'experience which is realized through consumption and promoted through advertisement. These are linked to the invention of plate glass, the spread of display windows and departmental stores, having choices in products—shopping is therefore reconstituted as a new bourgeois leisure activity not unlike going to a play or visiting a museum' (Stratton 1996: 28). In all these display techniques, the gaze of the observer or consumer is central.

We find that the importance of spectacle, display, and gaze arising from desire are crucial to identity formation in nineteenth and twentieth century continental thought. The importance of gaze finds its fullest expression in the psychoanalytical theory of Lacan (in the mirror phase) and is later taken up by film theorists for questions on spectatorship and viewing practices. Lacan (1949/2010) synthesizes Freud's sexual drive and Marx's politics and equates psychosexual prohibitions and repressions to political repression. He argues that the unconscious is structured like language and is political. Moreover, various laws derived from the dominant position of the signifier govern it. This dominant position of the signifier is identified with the male or the male gaze. Laura Mulvey (1975), in her early writings on film theory, argues that the gaze or the viewing pleasure of cinema follows the logic of male desire. She explains that film narratives are structured to diffuse the castration complex originating in the Oedipal stage of childhood development. Christian Metz, one of the pioneers of film theory, develops his argument on film viewing on the principle that the camera allows viewers to experience the illusion of wholeness, reminding them of their early childhood experience which is later shattered due to the realization of its lack (Plantinga and Smith 1999: 10–13).

This presumed human instinct to return to an earlier stage of childhood is widely accepted in contemporary film theory in India despite its derivation from and intimate relationship with the experiences of western modernity. Freud and Lacan, after all, were products of their times and cultures. Freud's writings were associated with the development of a new social organization—the nuclear family—during the turn of the nineteenth century. Both Freud's and Lacan's theorizations were integral to the new organization of the family and the spread of capitalism in the western world (Stratton 1996: 4–17). Plantinga (2009: 42) analyses the unquestioning assumption of desire as an unconscious drive in viewing practices associated with film theory and poses a critique:

In fact, the word 'desire' becomes a kind of clearing house for the entire panoply of unconscious and physiological drives, instincts, motivations, and pleasures. We are motivated by Desire when we are motivated by need of release of energy, by the death instinct, by sexual attractions, by homicidal impulses, by curiosity, by pleasure of looking.

Hence, the fundamental premise of desire (associated with unconscious drives) comes to occupy the position of a universal human condition in social theory. The experiential dimension of desire as fetishism and spectacle also takes root in Marxian analysis of commodities, but with a difference. Marx bestows commodities as possessing 'aura' and analyses it as 'commodity fetishism'. Marx (1867) shows how the capitalist system of exchange separates the commodity from the conditions of production and obfuscates the relations of production, which creates the 'aura' (Haug 1986). He argues that advertising invests commodities with particular cultural meaning where the commodity appears to entice the onlooker into buying the product. Haugh (1986) further develops this idea of aura into 'commodity affect' (more on this in Chapters 4 and 5). There is an interesting intersection of Freudian and Marxian understanding of fetish, in that they both take the idea from the anthropological tradition but go in different directions with their analysis of desire and experience.

Also influenced by a Marxian understanding of 'value' in a capitalist society, Walter Benjamin posits that 'aura' is what endows an object with authenticity. In an influential essay 'The Work of Art in the Age of Mechanical Reproduction' (1936), Benjamin argues that the loss of 'aura' is what differentiates the modern age of mechanical reproduction from an earlier classical age. Moreover, he argues that the loss of the ritualistic element of art due to technology has fundamentally changed the sensorium of art and consequently art is now integral to the practice of politics. Hence, the intersections of aesthetics and politics in analyses of culture, especially popular culture and media, have been critical for understanding modern subjectivities. Adorno and Horkheimer (1972) and the Frankfurt school thinkers were all deeply influenced by Benjamin and their debate is relevant even today. The Frankfurt school argued that popular/mass culture was a totalitarian industrial complex of domination whereas Benjamin saw popular culture as a potential arena of resistance. These early ideas regarding media and its power spawned many interpretations and theorizations including important works such as John Berger's *Ways of Seeing* (1972) and Neil Postman's *Amusing Ourselves to Death* (1985).

Gaze and Media

The fascination with gaze or scopophilia associated with fetishistic desire did not remain limited to cinema but spread through different kinds of media studies. Jonathan Crary (1990: 6) argues that in nineteenth century Europe a new kind of observer/spectator comes into being, different from a type dominant in the seventeenth and eighteenth century, for whom sight becomes disarticulated from touch. One can extend this argument to say that the sensorium of sight comes to dominate all other senses and the logic of the visual/textual preoccupies epistemological questions regarding subjectivity, desire, and the body in the nineteenth and twentieth century. The visual and textual explanation of the unconscious or the symbolic order becomes the dominant paradigm for analysing both the image and the moving image in products ranging from paintings and photography to films. Gradually we find that the 'screen' emerges as the dominant field of visual culture.

Kaja Silverman (1996) posits that the screen is the 'site' at which the gaze of a particular society is constituted and discusses the experience of gaze by its inhabitants as a visual regime of that society. Accordingly, she traces the relationship between a historical field of vision, its modern apparatus, and users (1996: 135). Wegenstein and Ruck (2011) develop their idea of gaze for analysing contemporary media by formulating the notion of the 'cosmetic gaze'. They show how different visual media inform and shape the gaze in historically specific ways, and also show how aspects of history are inherent in media practices today. They write (2011: 28):

> What we are calling cosmetic gaze is thus a gaze through which the act of looking at our bodies and those of others are already informed by techniques, expectations and strategies of bodily modifications; it is also a moralizing gaze, a way of looking at bodies as awaiting an improvement, physical and spiritual.

For analysing contemporary society, the authors re-conceptualize the fetishistic gaze of Freud and political gaze of Lacan as 'cosmetic gaze'. Here self-identity is equated to a sign or an image without any interior or psychic dimensions. As Joanne Finkelstein (1991) explains, in this new physiognomic discourse, it is not the face itself that becomes a sign, but self-identity is re-conceptualized as a sign or image. In discussing the televisuality of the new media such as the reality shows, Zylinska (2009: 37) proposes that the cosmetically improved bodies have become 'science fictional referent-less fetish images' that are looking at us from an unreal place but with a real imperative. The message is that one must change one's life, body, and sense of self to get a new sense of control that aims at happiness and success.

The relationship between the interior and the exterior resulting in the transformation of the exterior to change the interior are not new according to Wegenstein and Ruck (2011). It can be traced back to the concept of physiognomy (in ancient Greek philosophy) where there is a reciprocal relationship between beauty and goodness. In Aristotle's *Physiognomics*, the face is the essential emblem of this relationship between the body and soul. Johann Casper Lavator (1741–1801) derived his theories of soul from this Aristotelian idea and essentially promoted the essence of man as his soul and the body as the mirror of the soul.

The same idea permeated many areas of culture, art, and literature, and the scientists of the nineteenth century came to consider the biological body as the essence of man. However, Sir Francis Galton (1822–1911) broke from the divine understanding of the soul to a scientific method of analysis which ultimately helped him to promote eugenics (see Wegenstein and Ruck 2011). Wegenstein and Ruck (2011) argue that Lavator mapped his images or drawings onto an internalized normative screen based on a Christian world-order; Galton externalized the process with the use of a still camera and therefore entrusted a machine, a rational device, to make the ultimate judgment. The authors link the cosmetic gaze of the twenty-first century and the obsession with beauty and control to the inheritance of the Physiognomic approach (from Aristotle, Lavator, and Galton), which equated physical beauty with science and positive attributes. The underlining belief is that the authentic self of a person lies in the external appearance to be discovered through makeovers and transformation. It is based on the construction of self through technological means such as the photograph. Barthes writes (1981: 10, quoted in Wegenstein and Ruck 2011: 40):

> When I feel myself observed by the (camera) lens, everything changes: I constitute myself in the process of posing. I instantaneously make another body for myself. I transform myself in advance into an image … The photograph is the advent of myself as other …

But this understanding of the body as an object is limited. Many argue that if one is interested in a deeper transformation than at the cosmetic level to grapple with issues of identity, then one has to reach the register of affect and emotion. This reconstitution of self must work at the level of experience (see Malefyt 2007 who writes on how advertising targets emotion in consumer experience). Wegenstein and Ruck show how such emotional reconstitution is achieved through the reality shows of bodily makeovers. They use the example of the American show *The Swan*, a series that ran in 2004–5 on the television channel Fox (discussed by Zylinska 2009). But they contend that the show and generally shows like it propagate Eurocentric notions of beauty where all the contestants are homogenized into an average and then produced through technology as the perfect ideal beauty.

However, in the rapidly changing world of technology and new media, what constitutes 'gaze' is itself undergoing a transformation, collapsing the ideas of interior and exterior. We now live in a media-drenched world of screens where the visual spectrum is limitless and homogenization is impossible because it is so fragmented. Zizek quotes Lacan to describe the quandary of the twenty-first century experience of vision, where the field of vision has become an illusion without a blind spot. This illusive spot is the location from which the object returns the gaze, and when it disappears, vision is not possible and we are unable to gaze. 'The field of vision is a flat surface where reality is perceived as a visual hallucination' (Zizek 1997: 133). The real is now permeated and fragmented by machines where the opposition between subjectivity and objectivity is diffused. In this new order, the fetish images of the past are not only referent-less but are dissociated from all forms of representational codes.

Baudrillard (1983) argues that this is the end of perspective whereby simulation dominates our experience of reality. He presents this as a hyper-real state where the image no longer stands to represent the real. This condition is marked by a preoccupation with images over reality, where the image produces endless simulation without an origin (Baudrillard 1983). The questions of origin, genealogy, authenticity, and history have been associated with a modernist world of binary and hierarchical thought. Postmodern philosophers such as Deleuze and Guattari (1987) have argued that there is no division between the field of reality, representation, and subjectivity, but that these are all intersecting fields producing assemblages. Their conceptualization of 'rhizomatic culture' without a centre or roots articulates a process of constant becoming. In this postmodern view, subjects are released from their unitary and repressive modern identities to become 'desiring nomads'. In their theorization of the micropolitics of desire, where desire is not attached to any Freudian or Lacanian lack, radical change is brought about through 'line of flight' or liberation from desire itself.

This discussion shows that the analytical frameworks proposed by Hegel, Freud, Lacan, and Butler to explore desire and modern subjectivities also extend to media and film theories by Metz, Mulvey, Baudrillard, Deleuze and Guattari, Silverman, and others. However, they remain within the visual/textual realm of the symbolic order. The limitations of film theory and the obsessive textualization of subjectivity have been critiqued by film theorists such as Steven Shaviro in *The Cinematic Body* (1993). He argues that film theory superimposes on the cinematic apparatus the social theories of Marx, Freud, Lacan and Althusser in a reductive way, where percept and affect are subordinated to the law of textuality. He argues that over-textualization has produced a fear of images which can arouse corporeal reactions of desire, pleasure, fear, disgust, fascination and shame—in short a panoply of emotions. Hence, this kind of theorizing has produced knowledge and consciousness that is disengaged from materialistic affect and bodily sensations. I elaborate on Shaviro's (1993) arguments below to further explore how embodiment, desire, and experience entangle with filmic reception.

Affect and the Body

Shaviro (1993) pushes the debate on desire and subjectivity around the image and film reception to that between 'phenomenal presence' (immediacy of experience) and 'linguistic signification'. In short, between affect and cognition. He breaks from the standard film theory framework by arguing that the 'scientific' detachment of the great modernist belief (shared by structural formalism, psychoanalysis, and Brechtian aesthetic) is not applicable to films. He writes that such detached objectivity is not possible for film theory whose 'object' is not just particular films, but the very process of film viewing itself. The subjectivity of the theorist cannot be disengaged from this process but in fact is produced through the 'act of cinematic affect' (Shaviro 1993: 9).

Shaviro shows that classical film theory tends to suppress and regulate our visual experience by formulating the power of images within the boundaries of linguistic theory and patriarchal code and law. The image, in his view, does not symbolize 'lack', but expresses the excesses of the optical. From a Freudian and Lacanain theory of lack, he reorients film theory to the corporeal immediacy of the cinematic experience. He explains that deriving desire only from 'lack' reduces all power relations to the master narrative of castration or the subject's entry into patriarchal law. He takes Mulvey (1975) to task for proposing such a totalizing master narrative for all Hollywood mainstream cinematic experiences, since it offers no space for resistance. He posits that there is always a 'socios and a politics' to the imagined mythical Freudian and Lacanian moment when the 'symbolic order or system of norms is instituted in society, or implanted in the individual' (Shaviro 1993: 22). The child's entry into an affective sensory realm of the 'socios' is aptly described in the example below in a very different context.

The legendary Indian dancer Balasaraswati once said that those who wanted to understand her as a young child who was passionate about dance, should observe her grandson Anniruddha .... 'before he could speak or walk, raising one arm up from his crawling position, Ani would imitate the hands and facial expressions of his grandfather and mother while they sang' (Knight 2010: 17). The child learned how to emote and express himself through mimesis before he could speak. Shaviro further argues that the thinking in film theory is a result of a textual obsession in western epistemologies which privileges the text and claims there is no perception without cognition. He traces this line of thinking to Hegel's discussion of 'Sense-Certainty', which reduces the question of perception to a question of knowledge and equates raw sensations to a reflective consciousness of sense perceptions. In short, it ultimately denies the physicality of the body. Shaviro observes (1993: 25):

> It ignores or abstracts away from primordial forms of raw sensation: affect, excitation, simulation and repression and pain, shock and habit. It posits instead a disincarnate eye and ear where data are immediately objectified in the form of self conscious awareness and positive knowledge.

This understanding of perception is very different from Merleau-Ponty's theorization of the 'lived body' (1962). Leder follows Merleau-Ponty and extends the sensorimotor of perception to the visceral, the flesh and blood. It is through visceral and not just perceptual exchange, he argues, that 'the total interpenetration of the body and the world is realized' (Leder 1990: 205). Accordingly, film viewing is more tactile than contemplative and is experienced through the habit of sympathetic participation rather than mental attention. He injects the idea of mimesis in film viewing where we are brought into close contact with the image on the screen through a process of replication/copy and a material transfer (Taussig 1992). As a result, our viewing pleasure creates subjectivities that are not produced through repressing desires but self-abandonment and intoxication: 'the drives and enjoyments of the body cannot be equaled with the safety and stability of the ego. The masochism of the cinematic body is rather a passion of disequilibrium and misappropriation' (Shaviro 1993: 58). The classic mind-body dichotomy in western thought, which relegates the body to passive matter without intelligence, is the root of the reductive view of the corporeal sensory experience, he explains.

Shaviro traces a different kind of intellectual history for film theory, from Spinoza and Nietzsche (among others), where the body and thought are not opposed but related. The body in this view is not a container for the soul or inner mental being but a surface of 'inscription and reflection ... it includes everything from dress, cosmetic, skin, genitals and hair' (Shaviro 1993: 227). He strongly argues that in a postmodern world saturated with machines for mechanical reproduction, the machine used by the filmmaker can no longer be regarded as a tool to manipulate reality from a distance. In fact, distance is impossible and fragmentation and construction are not just modes of representation but processes of the real itself (Shaviro 1993: 37). The cinematic apparatus in the postmodern milieu is a mechanism for enhancing flatness or the mechanism of simulation. Thus, simulation is understood as a bodily event rather than an abstract spiritual one. That is, it is superficial in the sense that it engages the surface or the flesh rather than structuration of language or thought. Postmodern theorists such as Baudrillard and Jameson explain simulation in terms of freeing the sign from the referent and thus collapsing meaning. Shaviro claims film theory should be more about bodily affect and transformation than fantasy (psychoanalytical and other). The affect of sensory excesses is what film viewing brings to us, transforming, in turn, how we relate to our world. Marshall McLuhan (1994 [1964]) had observed that changes in media are changes in both human consciousness and the body. Due to changes in technology, we now perceive our bodies in new ways and our bodies are sensationalized, agitated and affected in new ways. In short, film viewers are 'chimeras, theorized and fabricated hybrids of machine organism' (Shaviro 1993: 264).

The notion of the scientific distanciation of the machine once associated with the photographic or filmic is further collapsed through new technologies of intimacy whether it is cyber media or reality television. Here the question is no longer about the image or screen as a mode of affective percept, but rather the loss of authentic affect due to the hijacking and mediatization of reality.

The penetration of technology in everyday life by the media apparatus of reality television is explored by Misha Kavka (2008). The long debate between exterior and interior, subjectivity and objectivity, real and mediated, is taken to another complex dimension through the ubiquitous presence of television reality shows. Kavka argues that it has been very easy to criticize reality television on the grounds that it is a misnomer. It misleads us by producing a sense of direct transmission, as if the viewers and participants are sharing a common unmediated space (a sense of 'being there'), when in reality it is all television and no reality (Kavka 2008: 22). She argues that reality television is not about realism in the ideologically grounded modernist sense but denotes an excess that belongs in the zone of affect, not cognition; this is different from the position held by Wegenstein and Ruck discussed earlier, but not unlike Shaviro's understanding of the cinematic apparatus. The reality effects of the mediated real are identified by her as 'constructed unmediation' which, she claims, often have greater immediacy than the world around us (Kavka 2008: 23). She cites Laurence Grossberg (1997: 135) who uses the phrase 'wild realism' in denoting affect, which is understood as being indifferent to meaning or signification. For instance, in reality television, rather than identifying with the feeling of the person on screen, the viewers identify with the affective situation, creating a 'community of affect'. Kavka (2008: 27) writes that: '"affective identification" is not a secondary, imitative or vicarious feeling, but rather an affective reality, something we are given to feel, which arises from the resonances played out across and through television screen'. Moreover, she distinguishes between emotion and affect and attaches affect to a spectrum of feelings before they have been identified to a specific object or source. Grossberg relates affect to mood and connects it to surface or skin rather than stemming from any deep model. In short, affect is content-less but emotion has meaning. Emotion occupies identifiable feeling states and exists according to cognition. Kavka calls affect a zone of potential emotion, which has not yet been differentiated.[1]

Therefore, in these analyses of subjectivity and desire, desire is neither repressed nor equated with power and reason, but is reconstituted as affect and sensations, and subjectivity as embodied and corporeal.

Anthropological Interventions and the Universal Subject of Desire

Visual Anthropology, Culture, and Emotion

The understanding of the intersections of affect, media, body, and technology in film and media studies remains bounded by universal human psychology, sensorium, and culture theory. This means that these theories in media studies have been developed for individuated western subjects for analysing advertising, photographic images, film, or television. Rather than being hemmed in by psychology or physiology, anthropologists have explored human emotions and feelings in terms of sociological and cultural processes by studying various non-western contexts. They have undertaken ethnographic fieldwork from a cross-cultural perspective to examine the complexities and textures of sensory experiences and feeling/affect/emotions in different settings. The process of 'thick description' (Geertz 1973) has enabled anthropologists to enter into continuing theoretical debates with other disciplines adding their own disciplinary insights. Through ethnography, they have

---

[1] Mazzarella suggests that affect is embodied and impersonal and produces a heightened sense of public intimacy. Mazzarella quotes Massumi (2002) in asking us to imagine social life in two simultaneous registers: an affective embodied intensity; and symbolic mediation and discursive elaboration. The intensity of the affective register is not pre-social here but asocial (292–3).

tried to reconstruct experience from an actor's point of view to describe and analyse the multilayered and culture-specific emotional and sensory experiences of communities.

Robert Levine (2007) cautions against reducing emotions to universal elements. Not unlike Geertz, who argued that just as we cannot speak without a particular language, if we leave out the particular cultural and psychological meanings of emotions by reducing them to their universal elements, we obliterate their functional significance in human communication and experience (Geertz 1973: 87; Levine 2007). Leavitt (1996) analyses how emotions involve meaning and feeling, mind and body, culture and biology and cannot be easily dichotomized into binary categories. A genre of analysis has developed in anthropology since the 1980s and 1990s around the explication of emotions as cultural categories (Rosaldo 1980; Abu-Lughod and Lutz 1990). The field of visual anthropology especially has focused on the multi-sensorial experiences involved in attempting to 'know' another culture. Although once associated with ethnographic films, the discipline (as conceived by Jay Ruby and Sol Worth in renaming the field as the Anthropology of Visual Communication) includes analysing all aspects of culture that are visible. They include non-verbal communication, the built environment, ritual, ceremonial performance, dance and art and material culture (Levinson and Ember 1996: 1345). However, as Ruby (1996) points out, anthropology as a field has been slow to respond to the centrality of the media in the formation of cultural identity and subjectivity in the second half of the twentieth century.

Early on, Franz Boas saw the tremendous potential of film technology as a tool of research for anthropologists (1944, Researching with a camera). His pioneering work in the fields of race and culture and their connection to behaviour and expressive forms was important in the development of visual anthropology. His interest in culture, body movements, and dance became important and allowed him to speculate about how to construct film footage (Ruby 1980, 1996). (Aside: not unlike how a dancer might think about how to choreograph a dance.)

Following his lead, Margaret Mead and Gregory Bateson produced films such as *Bathing Babies in Three Cultures* (1941) and *Trance and Dance in Bali* (1952) where they analysed human behaviour in intimate settings. Alan Lomax's choreometrics on cross-cultural studies of dance followed a similar notion of dance as cultural behaviour. Birdwhistell (1970) and Hall (1968) argued that the use of space was a form of culturally conditioned communication and psychologist like Ekman (1977) carried out research in the microanalysis of facial expressions and emotions.

Despite the establishment of somatic consciousness as being different from linguistic cognition by anthropologists such as John Blacking, linguistics was the heuristic device for grappling with non-verbal modes of communication, whether it is film, photography, dance, or ritual (Blacking 1977; Hymes 1962; Sol Worth 1981; Birdwhistell 1970; Kaeppler 1991). The 'body' as a component of visual culture entered the discourses of visual anthropology through the analysis of human movement. The body as a site for sensory and somatic research found its quintessential visual representation through dance (Farnell 2011). Anthropologists such as Ness (1992, 1995), Williams (1991), Mauss (1934/1973), and Douglas (1973) developed their own analogies for the 'techniques of the body' and the 'social-physical aspects of the body'. In all these intellectual developments, the fundamental epistemological and methodological problems for analysing the body remained the same. It was an attempt to go beyond interrelated conceptual binaries that stem from the mind-body dichotomy in western thought. Thus, emotion as a cultural expression remained somewhat relegated to a linguistic or cognitive dimension. Thomas Csordas illuminates this conundrum of pre-objective and objectified body through an example of the colonial encounter. He explains that the indigenous worldview did not make a distinction between the spirit world and the body. The native says to the anthropologist: 'we always acted in accord with the spirit, what you have brought us is the body' (Leenhardt 1979, 1949: 164, quoted in Csordas 1994: 6).

In recent years, several anthropologists have emphasized the importance of other perceptive faculties than the visual in many non-western cultures for understanding human behaviour and consciousness. It has shifted the discourse of culture as 'human behavior' to include 'human experience'. It has expanded the scope of visual anthropology to a different dimension of understanding culture; that is, as an examination of cultures and human subjectivities through the senses. Paul Stoller (1989), among others, has shown in his study of the Songhay of Niger, the importance of sensory awareness such as touch, smell, taste, and sound above the visual in understanding and tasting their way of life. Interestingly, as we will see in the next section, questions of the experiential dimension of the body and its relation to human subjectivity were at the core of Indian philosophical thought throughout its civilizational history. In most of this philosophy, sensory perceptions, affect, and tasting of emotion were key to analysing the human condition. Desire and the senses were wedded in these understandings of human consciousness, or simply put, consciousness was embodied.

Indian Philosophy, Embodied Aesthetics, Filmic Desire

Bodily Knowledge and Self

The discourses of desire, subjectivity, emotion, cognition, and the body have a completely different orientation in Indian thought. However, not unlike the west, consciousness and self-knowledge have been associated with the trope of 'desire' in classical Indian philosophy dating back to the second century BCE. Central to an Indian philosophy of subjectivity and desire is the corporeality of the body and a psychophysical consciousness that gives rise to affective/emotional responses that are liberating and not repressive, prohibitive, or cosmetic. In a humorous and insightful essay, Ramanujan (1989) asked the question whether there can be an episteme called the 'Indian way of thinking', and came up with some interesting characteristics. He argued that in Indian philosophical thought there was generally no distinction between self and other (non-self) or between exterior and interior. This is a direct contrast to much of western epistemological grounding, including the Hegelian dialectic of self and other (master and slave) for acquisition of knowledge, as discussed earlier. Second, Ramanujan argued that there is no Lévi-Straussian opposition between nature and culture in this worldview. He cites poetry in Tamil and from the Upanishads to underline how nature is contained within culture and vice versa. The third and significant point he makes is about the non-universal and con-text-specific meanings attached to all things human and non-human. He uses the concept of *jati* (translated as class/caste, genre, and species) as emblematic of this understanding of particularism. For instance, Ramanujan (1989: 46) writes:

> The main premise of Judeo/Christian ethics is based on such a prem-ise of universalization—Manu, who wrote Manusmriti [an ancient legal Hindu text that is part of the Dharmashastra, written between 200 BCE-200CE], will not understand such a premise. To be moral, for Manu, is to particularize—to ask who did what, to whom and when. Each class (jati) of man has his own laws, his own proper ethic, not to be universalized.

I will not explore the inequalities that result from this 'way of think-ing'. Many others have done that. Instead, I will explore how some of these attributes can be applied to a more general discussion on subjec-tivity and desire in classical Indian thought and its evolution. I am not arguing here that there is any kind of linear or systematic continuation of the classical tradition in Indian philosophy to modern times, nor am I proposing here a theory of rupture from ancient to modern. But rather, this is a deliberate effort not to slide into western epistemologies of subject and subjectivities as they relate to desire without taking into account some aspects of an Indian/Indic worldview. This worldview (or life-world) of an Indian way of thinking/feeling still persists albeit multiplicity, evolution, and modern incarnations. The question is: how do they persist and change, if they persist at all, and how are they relevant in understanding the contemporary subjectivities of a media-saturated world?

The questions regarding consciousness and subjectivity are complicated in India, as in many postcolonial nation states. Therefore, more specifically, I explore how some of these concepts evolved in a postcolonial modernity as the outcomes of an ongoing negotiation between tradition/past and modernity/present (this binary is obviously a simplification of complex processes of historical evolutions of ideas and practices and continuities and ruptures; so, this binary is simply a heuristic device). It should be noted that the discussion here is limited predominantly to a very selective classical Hindu canon (it is an Upanishadic worldview; of course, the category Hindu itself is a colonial construction and an amalgamation of a large variety of cultural and faith practices). The influence of Islamic thought, especially those emanating from the Sufi sect, is of utmost importance in the subcontinent as it intersected with the Hindu-bhakti traditions, but is explored in a very limited sense in this chapter.

In India philosophy, religion and aesthetics remain intertwined and do not fit neatly into separate or western-like categories. According to Doniger (2011: 185) there are six major approaches in Hindu philosophy: Critical Inquiry (Mimamsa), Logic (Nyaya), Particularism (Vaisheshika), Numbers (Sankhya/Samkhya), Yoga, and Vedanta (and its subsects Lokayatas and Charvaka). Sankhya philosophy dates back to the Upanishads and is important in the epic text Mahabharata, especially in the Gita. This is a dualistic philosophy that divides the universe into male purusha (spirit, self, or person) and female prakriti (matter/nature). There is an infinite number of similar but separate purusha. This is different from the philosophy of Advaita Vedanta that reads the Upanishads through the lens of the unity of the self (atman) and the cosmic principle (Brahman). There is a basic schism between these two approaches to knowledge, self, and a knowing god: the dualist and non-dualist (Doniger 2011: 505–6).[2]

In the classical Indian philosophy of Sankhya yoga, consciousness is not constructed as an opposition to 'other' as in Hegelian philosophy. It is 'self manifesting' and 'self luminous' and cannot be equated with the 'mind' of western epistemological traditions. In short, consciousness is not presented as an aspect of cognition (Rao 2011). Accordingly, the two principles *purusha* and *prakriti* exist in three different states. One of these states is bounded by desire expressed through prakriti. Prakriti is unconscious, matter, energy, creativity (the female principle), whereas purusha is consciousness/spirit and exists in multitude. Purusha bonds to prakriti through 'desire' and can exist in a pure state of consciousness or spirit. Although dualistic, it is not like the dualism of Descartes' mind/body, where the mind is supreme.

The most important aspect of this difference is the acknowledgement and the positive role of the matter or the materiality of the body (prakriti) in shaping experience and consciousness. This particular understanding of the body as a form of 'embodied mind' is explicit in yoga as the yoking of the mind and the body. According to Patanjali, a leading philosopher of yoga, it is the mind (*chitta*) which drives the

---

[2] The non-dualistic school of Vedanta spread through exponents of Shaivaite (Shiva-worshippers) and Vaishnavite (Vishnu-worshippers) schools such as Shankara from Kerala and Ramanuja from Tamil Nadu, as well as the Dvaitia or dualistic school of Vedanta through Madhvaharya in Karnataka (Doniger 2011: 506).

central functions of the body.[3] In his argument, the role of chitta which is the heart/soul involving the mental and the psychic, is distinguished from purusha that is consciousness or pure spirit. Carpenter (2008) writes that the concept of chitta is complex and all-encompassing; while it can be translated as mind or heart, it is not to be equated with the rational mind and cannot be isolated from feelings, intuitions, and memories. In later philosophical traditions such as Advaita Vedanta, the dualistic and complex metaphysics of purusha and prakriti are resolved by arguing for the fundamental unity of all things that includes our bodies and the world. This equation of the self and the universe dissolves all binaries between self and non-self, nature and culture, as Ramanujan (1989) observed. My focus is on this fundamental approach to the interdependence and interpenetration of mind and body in the construction of knowledge (jnana) in Indian philosophical thought.

Abhinavagupta, a Shaivite and a non-dualist writing in the tenth century, rejects the dualism of Sankhya philosophy. He posits that consciousness and self-awareness are not passive inner witnesses as Patanjali described in his yoga sutra, but consciousness is creative and manifests itself through the act of supreme will. Consciousness is like Shiva, who is both the creator and destroyer of the universe (Johnsen 2014). Shiva is a creative and active agent that not only refuses to take things passively but also has the capacity to reflect and know itself. There are some parallels with a Hegelian understanding in this formulation of thesis, antithesis, and synthesis, but knowledge or understanding of self is not reached through opposition or a set of dialectics. It is achieved through intense introspection and unification. Abhinavagupta argues that it is the arts that produce this undifferentiated state of consciousness: *ananda* (bliss)

---

[3] The yoga sutras of Patanjali were rediscovered in the nineteenth century due to the efforts of Swami Vivekananda. There are other prominent strands of yoga philosophy such as *hatha*, *tantric*, and *pashupata* that are not discussed here.

and *rasa* (aesthetic emotion). He re-theorizes the Natyashastra tradition of rasa (written between secondcentury BCE and second century CE) to a new state of consciousness of a liberated and enlightened soul. The braiding of philosophy, religion, and aesthetics in Indian thought finds its efflorescence in Abhinavagupta's *Abhinavabharati*. He writes (Locana 2.4, in Ingalls, Nasson, and Patwardhan, quoted in Schwartz 2004: 17) about aesthetics in the context of poetry in these words (that can be applied to other areas):

> Once rasa has been realized, its enjoyment (is possible), an enjoyment, which is different from the apprehensions, derived from memory or direct experience and which takes the form of melting, expansion, and radiance. This enjoyment is like the bliss that comes from realizing ones identity with the highest Brahman, for it consists of repose in the bliss which is the true nature of one's own self.

Indian Performance Theory

Theories of Sanskrit poetics are also reflected in the dramatic arts, music, dance, sculpture, painting, and architecture. In classical Indian thought, the artistic/creative experience is central to the realization of one's identity and ego, which is driven to subjugate itself or to rid itself of all duality and multiplicity. In order to reach this state, the distinctions between the body, mind, spirit, substance, affect and effect is collapsed (Schwartz 2004). Abhinavagupta argues that the nature or identity of the supreme being (Shiva/Siva) is contained within our own identity (Jiva). 'The Absolute (*Parama Siva*), as Abhinava visualizes it, is characterized by light (*prakasha*) and reflective awareness (*vimarsa*). Siva here does not simply refer to the personified deity but the consciousness underlying the totality of cosmic creation' (Jhanji 2007: 99). The individual identity is a smaller version of the supreme identity, and like it is also a conscious creative being. The importance of desire and creativity are explicitly linked to the formation of self-identity and subjectivity in Indian thought and we see the primacy of aesthetics and performance in all aspects of Indian life. Jhanji (2007: 102) writes:

> Thus we see here both theatre and life itself are liberating experiences once one becomes a *rasika*. A *rasika* of theater is the aesthete who sees the entire gamut of human emotivity emerge from and culminate into tranquility and the *rasika* of life is the mystic who sees the whole cosmic creation emerge from the same consciousness.

Perhaps it is no surprise then that Rabindranath Tagore found perfect subjectivity in the music-maker (as mentioned in the beginning of this chapter). Tagore's position is not unlike Merleau-Ponty's who argued that we diminish the substance of life in the world by thinking operationally, by defining rather than experiencing the reality. He envisioned the painter as the pathfinder to the 'there is'... a seeing-thinking from the inside (Stoller 1989: 39). Stoller goes on to quote Klee (Stoller: 1989: 38):

> In a forest, I have felt many times over that it was not I who looked at the forest. Some days I felt that the trees were looking at me. I was there, listening ... I think the painter must be penetrated by the universe and not penetrate it ... I expect to be inwardly submerged, buried. Perhaps I paint to break out.

We find in this quote a reflection of the merging and oneness in Indian thought, described by Ramanujan (1989) as the 'container and the contained' arising from deep philosophical reflections about introspection and subjectivity.

The conjoining of desire, subjectivity, aesthetics and performance is nowhere more pronounced than in the religious movement of bhakti that swept across all of India in the medieval period. The bhakti form of devotion personalizes the divine and embraces the enactment of dance and poetry to merge with it. Bhakti extends the concept of rasa enumerated by Bharata in Natyashastra and by Abhinavagupta, and places its source in *bhava* or a raw emotion that is fleeting (affect). Bhakti philosophy argues that intense personal emotion and bodily experience can lead to an impersonal state of heightened awareness, leading to the ultimate goal of transformation of the *atman* (the individual soul) to Brahman (the universal soul, rasa, ecstasy). But the cultural specificity of the experience is also significant as this form of consciousness is not accessible to the culturally uninitiated.

Although found in Shaivite and other sects, bhakti is primarily associated with Vaishnavism (followers of Vishnu, whose incarnation is Krishna). The rasa of bhakti or 'bhakti rasa' merges with *sringara rasa* (erotic love and longing) in a confluence of earthly and divine desire—a desire ignited through rapturous dancing and singing. Thus, the body is celebrated and recognized as a vehicle to express and to experience—everything from the ordinary to the divine. The narrative premise of bhakti centres on the Hindu god Krishna, who came down to earth to satisfy his desire for love. This desire for love is experienced through devotion or bhakti and sringara. The illicit relationship between Krishna and his lover Radha and Radha's reckless behaviour and self-abandonment are considered to be the truest expression of religious devotion and bhakti. This heightened emotional state also parallels feeling-states generated from the performance of music, dance, poetry and drama. Thus, in Indian thought, creativity and ecstasy or rasa are connected to fertility, and the understanding of creativity is sexual in nature.[4] Schwartz (2004: 48) explains:

> Indian traditions have not only incorporated physical desire and experience in their aesthetic theory, they have embraced them. The reasoning

---

[4] The corporeal connection between desire and sexuality has been exhaustively analysed by Freud. However, he disengaged it from materiality of the body or sexual drives to psychic drives.

is that if sexuality is responsible for life as we know it on the microcosmic plane, it must have its origins in the macrocosm, the divine realm, as well.

The *Kamasutra* (a Hindu text attributed to Vatsyayan, 400 BCE–200 CE) is also devoted to the exploration of sexuality where desire is expressed as Kama. Here Kama as a pleasure principle is not merely sexual but also sensual and is 'associated with music, good food, perfume, paintings' (Doniger 2011: 200).

Marglin (1985) analyses the unique relationship between sexuality, passion/emotion, devotion/bhakti, and 'sringara rasa' in her exploration of the culture and history of Odissi dance. She argues that sringara rasa is misleadingly translated as erotic emotion as it is an imperfect English translation of a Sanskrit concept. She offers instead the concept of 'embodied thought' which articulates 'sringara rasa' as an experience that is physical, emotional, and cognitive. Here the physical and emotional are not separate from cognition as we have seen in many western understandings, but the physical and emotional are united, simultaneous. So much so, that the 'nine rasa' states in Indian aesthetic theory are distinguished from the *sanchari bhava* states (which are simply fleeting moods without cognition, closer to 'affect' as discussed earlier). The context-specific taxonomies of aesthetic emotions or 'nine rasas' remind us of Indian philosophy's emphasis on particularism and multivalence. Furthermore, the metaphor of the 'container/contained' reflects the interdependence of various aspects of performance: deity and temple, temple and dance, dance and dancer, dancer and spectator. They all merge in the formation of rasa or the formation of pure consciousness (Marglin 1985; Schwartz 2004). A similar understanding is offered by Dimock who comments on the movement of consciousness from physical and sexual sensation towards achieving a 'blissful state of pure abstraction from all things physical to a state of samadhi' (Dimock 1998 [1966)]: 178 quoted in Child 2007).

It must be noted that bhakti evolved in a period of radical social change (primarily between fifteenth to seventeenth century) during which caste hierarchies were being challenged or rejected in favour of a more inclusive devotional identity in the image of the 'bhakta' or devotee. Bhakti was not contained within only a religious realm but informed a wider cultural and political realm. Its impact on aesthetics was significant through an outpouring of poetry, music, and songs, and it strongly influenced the 'structure of feelings' in the subcontinent. It continues to evolve and resonate in a variety of forms, shapes, and contexts, especially in the aesthetic realms of music, dance, and visual media. In fact, the modes of emotional experience and perception associated with bhakti and 'sringara rasa' are critically relevant for analysing the visual arts and culture in India due to their scopic dimension (note that the scopic here is not to be confused with Freudian and Lacanian 'lack' or scopophilia).

Islamic Influences

The gradual absorption of Persian aesthetics and traditions over hundreds of years within the Indian subcontinent is a subject of vast importance but is explored briefly here. However, their presence in Bombay/Bollywood films is undeniable, especially as they are expressed in the song and dance sequences through the confluence of bhakti and Sufi imageries. It is not farfetched to say that the syncretic traditions of Hindavi (medieval Hindi) and Urdu poetry found in the musical genres such as *qawaali*, *thumri*, and *ghazal* were developed in their modern incarnations in Bombay films (see Chapter 3). The qawaali form has undergone a metamorphosis in recent years and has emerged as a global-pop genre—so much so that Kavita Seth, a popular Bollywood singer, recently said in an interview that Bollywood has made Sufi music a separate genre.[5]

---

[5] Available at http://timesofindia.indiatimes.com/entertainment/hindi/music/news/Kavita-Seth-Bollywood-has-made-sufi-music-a-separate-genre/articleshow/50959159.cms

The Chisti Sufi order associated with Sufi practices in the subcontinent uses *qawaali* performances and the notion of *sama* (listening as meditation) as the path to spiritual transcendence (Kugle 2007). Amir Khusro (1253–1325) applied the conventions of Hindavi bhakti poetry to qawaali, where the image of pining for one's beloved in separation resonated with the Hindu bhakti of longing for Krishna by Radha. The most powerful embodiment of this emotion is encapsulated in sringara rasa/erotic emotion that is represented through dance. The dancing imageries, whether it be the ecstatic moment in Sufi qawaali where the body of the devotee soars upward or spins relentlessly, or in the ritual circular dance of raslila, represent the ecstatic moment of sublimation (Chakravorty 2005, 2009). It is perhaps no coincidence that both the *mujra* (traditional Kathak soiree by a tawaif/courtesan, which is a popular theme of Bombay/Bollywood films discussed in Chapter 3) and *majlis* (Sufi gatherings) invoke sensuous experiences and spiritual ecstasy through singing/dancing and mingles the sacred and the secular.[6]

Therefore, these examples of poetry, song, and dancing blur the boundaries between the sacred and the secular and allow the devotee/*bhakta*/*ashique*/lover to embody and experience 'sringara rasa'. In the context of Urdu and Hindi poetics, Behl (2012: 26) observes:

> Daaud's use of rasa allows us to specify a Sufi poetics of ordinate love. He links eroticism and ascetic transformation through the multiple meanings of 'juice' or 'essence' (rasa) that runs through Indian notions of poetry and praxis, reimagining the Chisti theology of 'ishq' (love) in richly suggestive language.

The blurring of the sacred and secular is also reflected in the absorption of the Persian secular *ghazal* form into the Hindu devotional *thumri* convention. *Ghazal* is known to resolve the tension between polar

---

[6] See Chakravorty (2009). Bombay films have also merged the two genres in beautiful song and dance renditions in films such as *Barsat ki Raat* (1960).

opposites that exists in the world. The conventions of the verses themselves pursue both highly structured rhyming and spontaneous outpouring of words in lines or verses that develop through stages. These conventions produce an expansion and contraction of meaning creating a constant movement akin to spinning/twist, which is the literal Arabic word root for *ghazal/gazal*. The imagery of spinning is reminiscent of Sufi dervishes and the essence of both is to join the lover/seeker with their eternal beloved. The lines below from Smith (2008: 8) give us the essence of Sufi philosophy encoded in *ghazals*:

> This expansion and contraction, feeling and thinking, heart and mind, combine to produce great tension and power that spirals inward and outward and creates an atmosphere that I would define as 'deep nostalgia'. This deep nostalgia is a primal moving force that flows through all life, art and song and produces within whoever comes into contact with it when it is consciously expressed, an irresistible yearning to unite the opposite it contains.

The pioneer ghazal queen and king Begum Akhtar and Mehedi Hussain, respectively, were known for the stylistic merging of thumri and ghazal in modern times. These gradual absorptions and accommodation of opposites in India resulting in Indo-Islamic syncretism might have had far reaching consequences other than aesthetic transformations and philosophical conversations. It perhaps led to the blurring of myth and history as experienced by its people summarized by Jafri (2010: 32):

> Sufism lies in its success in resolving the tension between the polar realities of the inward mystical experience or eternity, and the Sharia and history. Indian Sufism is heir to the martyrdom of al Hallaj, the sober spirituality of al Juniad, the ecstatic vision of bayazid ... and the spiritual flights of Vedantic monism.

Altogether Hindu bhakti and Sufi longing form a composite whole that increasingly has been fractured and distanced through politics.

Darshan

Visual transaction as an aspect of religious worship, embodiment, aesthetics, and philosophy, emerges as critical in the shaping of individual consciousness and subjectivity in Indic traditions (as can be expected by now, this is a very different approach from western psychoanalytical theories). The visual transaction is best understood through the concept of 'darshan'. Darshan is central to the relationship between the devotee or bhakta and the deity in Hindu worship. The visual pleasure of darshan is linked to the awakening of, rasa'but involves a much broader human sensorium than just the optic. Eck observes (1998: 14–15):

> Darshan, however, should not be conceptualized as an exclusively visual phenomenon. It is more than just the act of disembodied looking, it involves rather, imaginative and constructive activity, an act of making...
> it is not passive awareness of visual data, but an active focusing upon it, touching it. (Eck 1998: 15)

A transformative darshan necessarily involves reciprocal seeing. The visual privileging of perception through the eyes is reversed in rasa, where the distance between the observer and the observed is replaced by the direct sensuous experiences of tasting, touching, and feeling. The experience of rasa is 'sensuous, proximate, experiential, aromatic' (Schechner 2001: 29). It is gustatory and directly involves the body; it is associated with cooking, tasting, and inhaling the flavor.

The 'polyscopic' domain of viewing in India is not just limited to the idea of 'darshan'. Taylor (2002: 297) identifies two different trajectories of vision other than darshan. These intense penetrating gazes are *drishti* and nazar. They have poetic resonance dating back to the Persian-derived court culture of the Mughals. Many argue that the idea of darshan was embraced by the secular courtly culture of Islam in India where the *nawab* (king) held his court in similar visual transactions with his subjects. The term 'nazar' suggests the interlocking gaze between lovers or between devotee and deity (also a common imagery in Sufi qawaalis) and it signals a romantic initiation or a release of emotion.

Schwartz (2004) writes that India can be understood as an inherently sensual milieu of visual and gustatory delights. After all, rasa means taste and is associated with cooking with various condiments (*masala* or the mixing of the bhavas) to bring out a distilled flavour. The brilliant colors and the range of tactile sensations—sounds, smells, tastes—in festivities of music, dance, and rituals produce an experience of sensory overload.[7] It is interesting to contrast how the concept of 'taste' has been articulated in western thought. For instance, Hegel asserted that odor and taste were useless for artistic pleasure as 'aesthetic contemplation requires objectivity, without reference to desire or will, whereas things present themselves to smell only to the degree in which they are constituted by a process, in which they dissolve into the air with practical effects' (quoted in Stoller 1989: 25). Stoller goes on to argue that Kant, in his analysis of aesthetics in the Critique of Judgment (1790), articulated taste as an objective and rarefied distancing (1989: 23–4).

Christopher Pinney (2002: 335), who has written widely on India's popular visual culture, has described the interrelated visual rubric of chromolithographs, paintings, photographs, and cinema as an 'interocular field'. The continuity of frontal address in cinema (derived from the idea of darshan) and the iconic image of worship have been discussed by Chatterjee (2005: 90–6). She cites many popular Hindi films from the past to the present where this visual tradition has been employed. The gaze is aurally and symbolically embellished in the lyrics and music of film songs, heightening the emotive quality of nazar. The overlapping

[7] Here the Sanskrit idea of *Dhvani* as resonance/sound/suggestion also comes into play in experiencing rasa (for an elaboration on the poetics of *Dhvani*, see Rustomji 1989).

meaning of darshan and nazar is summarized in the following passage
from Bhatti and Pinney (2011: 226):

> The sense of vision is more than simply looking, as a dimension of the
> sensorium through which the viewer seeks to feel, touch, and hold the
> image through the gaze and other bodily senses recalls the multisenso-
> rial aspects of darshan and is something that the polyscopic visualities of
> South Asia demand, and viewers of the film expect.

We see here that exploring desire and subjectivity through the lens of
classical or medieval Indian philosophy and aesthetics brings us closer
to a corporeal understanding of human consciousness associated with
the 'cinematic body' (as in film theory) or sensory embodiments (as in
anthropology).

Indian Film Theory and Darshan / Gaze

How has Indian cinema accounted for or incorporated the classical
and medieval Indian ideas on rasa, bhakti, and darshan, and, more nar-
rowly, how have analysts of Indian cinema accounted for them? From
its inception, Hindi cinema has negotiated the dialectic of tradition and
modernity in its construction of a national narrative. Nandy (1998)
uses the notion of desire and fantasy within a psycho-social context to
analyse popular Hindi cinema's wide-ranging subjects and the formation of middle-class subjectivity. Vasudevan (2000) critiques Nandy for
analysing the modern subjectivity of filmic characters within traditional
social mores, against the atomization of modernity. Many of the earlier scholars of film studies in India were preoccupied by cinema's role
in forming the citizen-subject within a national narrative of identity
formation.

Madhav Prasad (1998), in a seminal work on Bombay films, employs
a combination of Marxist, psychoanalytical, and 'darshanic' models to
analyse Indian viewership. However, he emphasizes the importance of

the theatrical/performance 'model of direct address' and 'frontality' as the continuing conventions in Hindi cinema. Gehlawat (2010) critiques Prasad (1998) and Vasudevan (2000) and others for using primarily the 'devotional paradigm' of darshan for analysing the implied viewer's relationship to Bombay films. He argues that this kind of theorizing presupposes a primarily homogenous Hindu audience in place of an Indian audience and their varieties of religious beliefs. He cites Metz's characterization of the theatrical media as different from the filmic media, which ultimately produces different constructions of spectatorship. On the other hand, Shaviro's debunking of psychoanalytical theory (discussed earlier) and his emphasis on affect and the importance of bodily sensation in the construction of the viewer's relationship to the moving image draws film closer to a visceral theatrical experience rather than the so-called distance, lack, or absence associated with conventional film theory. Shaviro argues that innovations in technology have fundamentally changed the relationship between the cinematic apparatus and the body. However, in arguing against the construction of Indian cinema in the image of national identity, Gehlawat proposes a postmodern paradigm for Bombay/Bollywood cinema that embraces the idea of 'impersonation' (Chakravarty 1993). He extends Chakravarty's idea to argue for a more eclectic framework, one that goes well beyond the construction of a national narrative, for the subversion of Indian film theory. Gehlawat (2010: xxvii) writes:

> By focusing on the unique filmic components of the Bollywood film, such as the frequent use of playback, sound and lip-synching, or the multiple scenic backgrounds and settings employed in song and dance sequence, a simultaneous shift from a religious to a postmodern perspective becomes possible.

He argues that the concept of 'impersonation' as used by Chakravarty can disrupt playfully the so-called narrative of the nation and national identity. The idea of 'impersonation', which Chakravarty uses for her analysis of Hindi films, is derived from an indigenous performance genre of India's precolonial past. Its easy conflation into a postmodern perspective of 'play' as suggested by Gehlawat is a decontextualized assertion. Moreover, Gehlawat's narrow understanding of darshan only within a Hindu religious framework and his invocation of 'ecstasy' (through Baudrillard) and masala without any reference to Indian performance theory is Eurocentric. However, his focus on the song and dance sequences of Bombay/Bollywood film is timely, as it underlines the paradox of their ubiquitous presence on screen and conspicuous absence in formulating Indian film theory (Gehlawat 2010). This is an acknowledgement of the primary importance of performance in shaping the filmic narrative. He (2010: xxiii) writes:

> More than any other element in Bollywood film, the song and dance functions as a reframing device, allowing films and their characters to rearticulate their visions, desires, and, indeed, viewers' understanding of both.

The scopic intersections (interocularity) of modern media such as cinema and television with older traditions of music, dance and theatre weave a highly complex matrix of the performance-visual continuum where several spheres of meaning exist in tandem. In the contemporary digital world, the visual and sensory aesthetics of the past (Walter Benjamin's 'aura') derived from Indian philosophical, religious and secular traditions entangle with modern technologies of imaging such as photography, cinema, television and other media. Bombay cinema from its inception embraced the centrality of music, dance, ritual and festivals in Indian life (to be elaborated in the next chapter) which still are a vibrant centre for the intersection of technology, culture, and aesthetics. Contemporary popular television genres such as dance reality shows are part of the same scopic landscape, in which 'traditional' dance practices that were reinvented as 'classical' and 'folk' renegotiate the new technologies and contemporary consumer culture. The paradoxical relationships between new media forms (such as dance reality shows) and traditional practices of the past demand a simultaneous rejection, acceptance, and adaptation to the forces of postcolonial modernity. I explore these complex dynamics in creating contemporary Indian subjectivity and new desires throughout the rest of the book.

Screens and Dances

The philosophical engagements of the previous chapter traced multiple theoretical traditions from the east and west to arrive at the valence of desire and subjectivity in Indian dance and media. It highlighted some of the key philosophical concepts that frame the subject in western and Indian thought with a special focus on the changing notions of subjectivity as our lived experiences become increasingly integrated with a technology-driven visual culture. In order to explore the new forms of subjectivities that are forged through the interactions of various media technologies such as cinema, video, the internet, and television, and their relationship to traditional expressions of visual culture such as dance, ritual, festival, I focus on the emergence of new televisual genres such as dance reality shows in India. However, rather than looking at it as a global phenomenon, which it is, my explorations situate it within localized Indian contexts. In other words, I argue that in order to understand the depth of these new media phenomena, postmodern ideas of 'flattening multiplicity' and 'rhizomatic culture' (Deleuze and Guattari 1987) are powerful but inadequate to explore memory, experience, and subjectivity in a culturally meaningful and embodied way.

In order to excavate the sensory experience of desire as it pertains to technology and visual culture, it is necessary to ground these ideas in specific histories and ethnographic contexts. Thus, dance reality shows in India may use the concept from television reality shows as they emerged in the west, but they are deeply grounded in the visual and sensory culture of India and its all-pervasive media apparatus: Bombay films (renamed Bollywood in the 1980s). My investigation of the dancing in dance reality shows begins with uncovering this indigenous logic of the visual genre by tracing it within the song and dance sequences of Bombay/Bollywood films (I am referring to the dancing in Hindi films that is always accompanied with song as 'song and dance sequences' following the work of Gopal and Moorti 2008).[1] The song and dance sequences in Bombay films were forerunners of the music video industry both in the west and in India and the intimate connections between the west and the east or Hollywood and Bollywood are best understood as a narrative both of homogenization and the specificities of culture and aesthetics.[2]

---

[1] An informative blog on Hindi film song and dance sequences is cinemanrtiyagharana, available at http://cinemanrityagharana.blogspot.com.

[2] Kaur and Sinha (2005: 15) study this overlap that produces common ground and digressions between the two industries and how they are studied: 'Bollywood's integration to films studies has brought it closer to conceptual frameworks developed for Hollywood narrative technique (audience voyeurism, narrative techniques, and so on), and consequently Hollywood's cultural capitalism is mapped, consciously or unconsciously, onto that of India's commercial cinema. One of the fundamental differences between Hollywood and Bollywood is that the former pushes world cultures towards homogenization, whereas the latter introduces in those cultures a fragmentary process.' Also, see Gehlawat (2010).

The intersection of tradition, technology, and the imaginings of the citizen-subject in modern India finds its fullest expression in Bombay films. The main concern for the early scholars of film studies in India revolved around questions of representation, framing, and the construction of spectatorship and citizenry.[3] I begin by examining the conceptual framework of desire and subjectivity as it relates to the nation and citizen in the song and dance sequences in Bombay films. I construct here a selective genealogy (or an ad hoc genealogy as the archive is an inexhaustible treasure trove) of film dances. My intention is not to produce an exhaustive list of the song and dance sequences that were ever created, but to selectively analyse a few important ones that gave new directions to the evolution of the visual/ 'interocular' field (Pinney 2002), in which Indian dance belongs today.

The chapter is divided into three sections. In the first section, titled 'The Desiring Subject of the Songs and Dances', desire (once again) forms the theoretical lens to explore the song and dance sequences as aspects of both *aesthetic* and *material* desire in shaping the Indian citizen-subject. The second section, 'Bombay Filmi Nach to Bollywood Dance' explores the song and dance sequences that negotiated indigenous

---

[3] However, the semiotics of such analyses was based on a universalized Indian subject, a spectator without particular location or identity. The critique of this singular approach to readings of film narrative has come under scrutiny and is succinctly summarized by Sengupta (2005: 137): 'The atelier of the cameraman, that messy studio floor with its cabling, its scaffolds, its grease, its heavy machinery and its nightmarish production schedule is one of that the film historian and film theorist of Indian cinema have by and large never stepped into. They have rarely crossed the border to the terrain of trying to understand the conditions of practice. The tools of their understanding, far removed from the concrete realities of the industrial production apparatus of cinema are forged into parlors of abstracted narrative analysis and an ahistorical aestheticism that has to do with folkloristics than film studies.'

aesthetics and western cosmopolitanism to create an enduring tension between tradition and modernity.[4] The third section titled 'Mixing Bhavas to Remix' analyses the fragmentation and emergence of the new aesthetics of 'remix' in Bollywood. The three sections establish a genealogical link between the dancing we see on TV reality shows and in Bombay/Bollywood films.[5] The link is traced through the sensory dimensions of desire, emotion, and affect.

The Desiring Subject of the Songs and Dances

'Desire' as articulated and embodied through the songs and dances in Bombay films of the past belonged to the mythopoetic world of Bhakti and Sufi love mysticism. The music and dance were imbued with rasas, such as bhakti rasa (devotional desire) and sringara rasa (erotic desire) that alluded to the classical aesthetics of India's past. Although many of the song and dance sequences were influenced by Uday Shankar (who gave a new dimension to the classical rasa aesthetics) and some were derived purely from western forms (to be discussed later), the songs and dances were generally associated with traditional Indian aesthetics and philosophy even while negotiating an aesthetic of western modernity. Some of these philosophical underpinnings have been discussed in Chapter 2. It is no surprise then that Indian dances have been an important feature of Bombay cinema from its inception. Both have been integral to the project of nation-building and fostering a sense of collective national identity (as discussed briefly in the previous chapter). Both cinema and dance have used similar cultural and aesthetic codes for making meaning, creating emotion/affect, and constructing a modern identity through the poetics of rasas which established a sense

---

[4] The regional industries such as Tamil, Telugu, or Bengali films produce a kind of vernacular-modernity that is different than Bollywood.

[5] Parts of this chapter have been discussed in Chakravorty (2016).

of cultural continuity with a classical past. Classical and folk dances ranging from Kathak and Bharatanatyam to Nautanki and Raslila have been the staple of Bombay films. Sangeeta Shresthova (2003, 2011), for example, has analysed the peculiar cyclical migration of film dance from a medium that was influenced by existing performance traditions of classical and folk to a legitimate form of staged theatrical dance today called Bollywood.

In Hindi films such as *Devdas, Guide, Pyaasa, Kinara* and others, the soul's longing for union with the divine was imagined in song and dance sequences that expressed a lover's desire for his beloved. These sequences often evoked images of Radha and Krishna or Laila and Majnu, transforming the screen to a mythic land of love mysticism. The songs and dances connected the audience to the cultural habitus of deeply felt emotions of longing and desire encoded in the aesthetics of bhava and rasa. They helped to create a sense of tradition and continuity in the new narrative of nation and identity within a postcolonial context. These dances and songs resonated with the ethos of *parampara* (tradition), a multifaceted word that refers also to a specific method of dance practice, or social organization, or transmission of knowledge. Many films directly incorporated this special training relationship between student and teacher (popularly known as the *gurushisya parampara* or *ustad-shagird* tradition) in their plot. Films such as *Jhanak Jhanak Payal Baje, Ganga Jamuna, Surasangam, Shankarabharanam,* and *Umrao Jaan* use this specific practice-oriented disciplining of the body in narrating stories of dancers and musicians (Chakravorty 2009a). Many famous dancers and choreographers appeared on the silver screen, including Gopi Krishna, Waheeda Rahman, Vaijayantimala, Helen, Kamal Hassan, Hema Malini, and Madhuri Dixit, to name a select few.

Born out of Parsi theatre, which blended the local idiom with received colonial aesthetic forms, Bombay cinema has been a fulcrum of creative hybridity (Mishra 2002: 1–33). It has grappled with two competing modes of representation: melodrama (derived from traditional aesthetics of dance and theatre) and realism. This negotiation has reflected the larger cultural discourse surrounding tradition and modernity in India as both continue to shape the narrative of democracy and citizenship (Prasad 1998).

In the last two decades, due to globalization, new technology, and the democratization of consumption, a decentralized and fragmented visual field of images have replaced an earlier bounded aesthetic cultural identity. The embodiment of erotic desire through music and dance (such as sringara rasa, encapsulated in *chherchhar* or amorous play in song and dance) has transformed to a new kind of desire—from love and mysticism it has evolved to a new aesthetics of eroticism. Bombay cinema, in turning into Bollywood, has created some stunning images of dance through new digital technologies, costumes, sets, and dance techniques. Bollywood songs and dances have pushed the commodification of images of dance and dancing bodies to a new material and aesthetic dimension of desire. This new kind of voluptuous desire is aspirational and consumerist, associated with markets rather than spirituality, mysticism, tradition, or nation.

Despite the stark changes in aesthetics and content, scholars of cinema argue that Bollywood (like Bombay cinema) continues to be the sole model of national unity in a country fragmented by regionalism, caste, and communal politics (Chakravarty 1993; Gopal and Moorty 2008). One can argue that the song and dance sequences are the repository of India's pulsating, paradoxical, protean national soul as it negotiates the forces of markets and modernity. The song and dance sequences, recently reinvented as 'item numbers', offer myriad possibilities of heightened desires and aspirations to be an ideal Indian today, and at the same time be a cosmopolitan citizen who is comfortable with an ever-expanding visual field. These sequences function as a bridge between past aesthetic codes associated with classical and folk dances and new ones from MTV, Broadway musicals, music videos, and postmodern choreography. Simply put, Bollywood song and dance sequences form a quintessential locus of the complex negotiation between India's past and its desire to be a modern democracy and stake a claim in global popular culture. The song and dance sequences function as sites for ushering in new understandings of culture, power, democracy, and citizenship (Thussu 2013). Booth (2000: 128) traces the changing conventions and shifting meanings of song and dance representations in Bombay cinema from earlier times:

> The visual images in these scenes have filled Indian theaters with a stylized vocabulary of dance and gesture ranging from maidenly brushes of the 1940's Lila Chitnis to the brazen bump and grind of the 1990's Madhuri Dixit. Thus, when a song and dance scene appears in a film (of course, its very appearance is a narrative convention) the conventions inform not only the musical, visual and kinesthetic content, but also types of meaning one can expect and the coded elements that will be used to construct that meaning.

In the past two decades, a paradigm shift has taken place in the musical, visual, and kinesthetic content of the song and dance sequences that have challenged the established norms, codes, and meanings. The earlier codes were predominantly drawn from the mythopoetic semiotic world of *Bhakti* and *Sufi* love-mysticism as discussed before; they have been replaced by gyrating bodies endlessly on display creating overtly sexualized commodity transactions. The latter roles, once only reserved for 'vamps' (played by Helen or Nadira in the past), are now coveted by leading heroines. As the song and dance sequences have taken on a new format and movement idiom, they have increasingly been dissociated from the plot (as we will see in the discussion below). Consequently, their commodity status is heightened. They now create the 'repeat value' of a film and circulate as music videos and 'item numbers' on television channels, iTunes, and YouTube. They function like franchise productions, transforming the notion of cultural production into the notion of a rhizomatic culture, where one product leads to other kinds of related merchandise (Deleuze and Guattari 1987). The rise of the multiplex as part of the production system is an aspect of the same rhizomatic multiplication.

I propose that the term 'remix' captures these new practices and aesthetics of Bollywood dance. 'Remix' as a cultural practice and aesthetics ultimately represents the seductive desire of the markets. In short, 'remix' is an expression of consumerist desire expressed through the hyper-visualization of commodity images or 'commodity aesthetics' (Haug 1986). Bollywood dance, I argue, is a potent engine for producing this kind of euphoric aesthetic delight and sensory gratification in contemporary India. With its slick bodies and designer clothes, Bollywood dance enables the dancer and the viewer alike to produce themselves as individual consumers disconnected from their social class, family, or community. In this new consumerist phase of Indian modernity, 'erotic desire' or sringara that is part of the *bhava/rasa* aesthetics of Indian music and dance is transformed into a set of tantalizing images associated with the aesthetics of commodification, such as in advertising products (Chakravorty 2008). In recent films, 'item numbers' represent the further crystallization of the commodity images that are aspirational and spectacular in nature. The 'aspirational images' are associated with advertising (of affect/sensations) that creates the desire in the onlooker to consume or buy a product. It also inspires a personal transformation not unlike the concept of 'cosmetic gaze' (as discussed in Chapter 2 in the context of dance reality shows such as *Swan*). These concepts can also extend to valuing a certain lifestyle or geographical area. Mazzarella explains (2003: 102):

> The statement that objects or images may be 'aspirational' implies that an orientation toward such objects or images indicates a desire for personal transformation, in line with a widely diffused and thus generally recognized index of advancement. Aspirational qualities appear, on the

face of it, to be inherent properties. Thus marketing theorist Davis Aaker writes: 'The brand [Nike] is very aspirational in the sense that wearing Nike represents what the users aspire to be like rather than their current self-image' [Aaker 1995; 514–550]. Aspirational qualities are, moreover, associated not only with particular brands but also with whole quasi-geographical imaginaries.

This form of aspirational desire of a new generation of Indians, I argue, is writ large on the canvas of films such as *Dhoom 2* or *Don 2*. Now the heroes and heroines exude the cosmopolitan aura of western fashion models with their perfect bodies, stylish clothes and accessories, fair skin, and golden hair highlights. But the cultural products coming out of Bollywood are not homogenous. Directors such as Sooraj Barjatya are interested in creating films that harken back to past notions of culture and tradition in an auto-exoticizing mode. There is a market for everything, from tradition and invented tradition to cosmopolitanism or imaginations of cosmopolitanism.

Bombay Filmi Nach to Bollywood Dance

In order to trace the evolution of the aesthetic codes of the song and dance sequences in Bombay/ Bollywood films, I analyse a select list of song and dance sequences below. This exploration of the aesthetics of song and dance sequences from the past to the present not only maps their evolution from Bombay cinema to Bollywood films (or Filmi naach to Bollywood dance) but traces a trajectory of embodied emotions in music and dance.

The kind of staging, lighting, sets, dancing, music, and choreography that became identified as the Bombay film song and dance sequence represented a paradigm shift in the history of the modernization of Indian dance and music. It is in Indian film dances that the idea of choreography (a concept used in Euro-American dances for organizing space) was indigenized and Indianized. The screen, camera, and lighting provided the main thrust for this process of re-imagination of dance. Innovation in Indian concert dances that originally came out of the temple and court traditions was focused on 'time' involving *tala* (rhythm) and *laya* (tempo) rather than 'space' and choreographic concepts (discussed in Chapter 4). In fact, the word 'choreography' was seldom used in the past and its popularity today is an aspect of a global dance parlance imported from the west.

However, Bombay films were instrumental in giving birth to a new genre of dance that used space and time to mark a new Indian form that departed from the usual aesthetics associated with classicism. This form celebrated hybridity rather than the narratives of purity and nation-hood associated with the revival of classical Indian dances (Chakravorty 1998; Coorlawala 2004). Several early filmmakers argued that the ubiquitous presence of song and dance in Bombay films was a vehicle for indigenous self-expression, so as to keep the cultural forces of foreign influences at bay. The song and dance sequences during this time drew on traditional and regional folk theatre and dance forms such as 'raslila', 'nautanki', 'jatra', and 'tamasha' to welcome a hybridization of narrative technique. The ingredients also included classical Sanskrit plays, like those of Kalidasa dating back to the fifth century AD (Nihalani, Gulzar, and Chatterjee 2004: 13)

The mixture of moods and emotions at the core of popular Hindi cinema was an extension of these classical aesthetics encoded in the *navarasa* (nine rasas) discussed in the famous dance and drama treatise *Natyashastra*. But at the same time, the spectacle and the song picturization connected the song and dance sequences to preexisting theatrical forms in colonial India such as Parsi theatre. Kathryn Hansen has written about Parsi theatre and its propensity to consolidate disparate local performances into a pan-Indian style (Hansen 2003; Gupta 2005). Gopal and Moorti (2008) explain that the emphasis on spectacle and song in conjunction with an enduring connection to older genres created a new aesthetic of the 'modern'. A good example of this movement across genre and media is the film *Indar Sabha* (Figure 3.1), which was based on a printed text (a play) that became one of the first talkies.

The first sound film in India, *Alam Ara* (1931 [see Figure 3.2]) by Ardeshir Irani, successfully blended music, song, and dance as central aspects of the film. Like *Indar Sabha*, it too was a popular fantasy play turned into cinema. The play was written by Joseph David and the film

FIGURE 3.1   Poster for *Indar Sabha*
Courtesy: NFAI, Pune.

FIGURE 3.2   Still from *Alam Ara*
Courtesy: NFAI, Pune.

was an international venture. In the 25th year souvenir of the magazine *Indian Talkie* (1931–56) published by the Film Federation of India, the release of *Alam Ara* (1931) was described as the birth cry of the talkie. The film was replete with song and dance sequences; its advertisement read 'All Talking Singing Dancing'. But the transition from silent to talkie was not without struggle. Especially the performance of song and dance from staged products to their representation on screen was seen as a loss in one dimension but a gain in editing and manipulation. Dandayudapani (1956) discusses the technique in the souvenir of *Indian Talkie*, observing that: 'Initially the music directors had to compress the song into one of three minute duration without the loss of its charm and emotional appeal; The dance director then rehearsed the artist, choosing the movements and gestures and it had to be rendered piece by piece.' The film was shot on the single Tanar system camera that recorded both image and sound simultaneously, a technical feature that restricted flexibility in the composition of a scene. This problem was rectified in *Indar Sabha* by J.J. Madan a year later (Gopal and Moorti 2008:

20). By then *Alam Ara* had proved that talkies had come to stay in India. With the introduction of the playback system in 1935, a more elaborate staging of the dances became possible due to greater mobility of the dancers (Gopal and Moorti 2008).

The director and choreographer who revolutionized dancing on screen and merged cinematography with choreography was the modern dance pioneer Uday Shankar in his film *Kalpana* (1948). The film was shot at Gemini Studio and was written, directed, and produced by Uday Shankar. It starred Amala Shankar (Uday Shankar's wife), the Russian ballerina Simkie, and Padmini, a dancer who made her debut in that film. Although not considered a typical Bombay film, *Kalpana* was groundbreaking for giving a cinematic treatment to the traditional dances of India. Uday Shankar reinvented the 'rasa' aesthetics for the camera. His novel approach to dancing for the camera required a complete readjustment of dance movements but without compromising its embodied aesthetics. In addition, for the first time in Hindi films, it imagined the male protagonist as a dancer. The storyline was autobiographical and revolved around a dancer's dream of setting up a dance academy and the rivalry between two women, Kamini and Uma, for his love. The striving of an artist to realize his dreams was dramatized in a lyrical montage of dramatic sequences and images. The advertisements for the film in the magazine *Film India* read: 'A feast of music, melodrama, and dance in a story that touches you to the core' (Patel 1948: 50). Despite its tepid reception in the box office, the reviews were full of excitement. In the same magazine, in an article titled 'Kalpana Is an Artist's Dream in Celluloid', the reviewer wrote: 'The dream of love, the labour and machine ballet, the spring festival of dances … these are the highlights that would have done honour to the most experienced film director … the Shantarams, Nitin Boses and Mehboobs' (Patel 1948: 50).

Kalpana displayed the indigenous heterogeneity of Indian dances (both classical and folk) to weave a tapestry of sensuous images. For the first time, Indians witnessed the wealth of their dance traditions from Rajasthani folk to Kerala Kathakali. The film introduced to Indian dance the ideas of choreography, staging, and movement—designed specifically for the camera. The imaginative camera use and cinematography were striking in the ways that they split the screen to bring into focus both the dancing body and the drumming hands, establishing the intimate and interdependent sensory relationship between dance (movement) and music (sound) in Indian aesthetics. Music director Vishnudas Shirali explored the orchestral possibilities of Indian music with great imagination.

Uday Shankar's use of stage sets and lighting created an aesthetic context for both dance and films that was new and modern in India. The famous 'labor and machine' sequence was stunning in the way it cohered the movements of the machine with human movements and produced a commentary on the mechanization of humans. This somber sequence contrasted with a scene of spring that celebrated India's diversity by employing various folk songs with dances. Drums were used as stage props and dancers unexpectedly sprang out of them (a scene repeated and made famous in the hit film *Chandralekha*, 1948). Indonesian Gamelan was used to enhance the strong musicality of the dance sequences. The unusual lyrical quality of *Kalpana* rendered it a kind of performed poetry rather than a conventional story. Despite the limitations of the drama and acting, the film created a rhythmic coherence of shots, scenes, and sequences (Gopal and Moorti 2008: 26). Simkie, the Russian ballerina from Uday Shankar's troupe, also choreographed for this film.[6]

Shankar's influence on Hindi films was far-reaching. The German expressionism and chiaroscuro effects introduced by Uday Shankar

---

[6] For an in-depth discussion on Uday Shankar's *Kalpana*, see Sarkar Munsi (2011).

permeated the work of important later Bombay film directors such as Raj Kapoor and Guru Dutt. Gopal and Moorti (2008: 26) write that Uday Shankar's exploration of 'semi expressionist angles and chiaroscuro effects ... become[s] a model for the dream sequence in later movies such as *Awara* (Vagabond) by director Raj Kapoor.' *Kalpana* also became a model for modern Indian dance, rejecting some of the puritanism associated with the revival of classical Indian dances. It was a dreamscape of Uday Shankar's desire for a national identity that was deeply Indian and modern. In Gopal and Moorti's summary judgment (2008: 26): 'Uday Shankar uses traditional dance as a metaphor for the aspirations of an independent India.'

Chandralekha (1948 [Figure 3.3]), directed by S.S. Vasan, was another iconic film that created cinematic spectacle through its music and dance sequences.

However, unlike *Kalpana*, the main goal of the film was to provide entertainment rather than carry out artistic experimentation. The

FIGURE 3.3   Still from *Chandralekha*
Courtesy: NFAI, Pune.

choreography in *Chandralekha* established a new aesthetic of visual vistas, spatial arrangements, and collective movements that was influenced by *Kalpana* but with a difference. The collaborative choreography by Jaya Shankar, Mrs Rainbird, Natnam Natraj, and Niranjana Devi incorporated Indian and western dance forms, including circus and trapeze to create a global hybrid choreography that could be considered a forerunner to Bollywood dance (Gopal and Moorti 2008). Since both *Kalpana* and *Chandralekha* were shot in Gemini Studio, *Kalpana* heavily influenced Vasan's focus on choreographic and cinematographic confluence.

Chandralekha was the first film to get an all-India distribution; a big budget extravaganza that became the first all-India blockbuster. The story was also a love triangle like *Kalpana*, but this time *Chandralekha*, played by T.R. Rajakumari, was a female dancer, and the two males who desired her were brothers. In the choreography, the use of close-up shots that highlighted the articulation of bodily movements such as hand gestures, eyes, and head tilts were a direct nod to classical Indian dances. At the same time, the orchestral music using drums, *kartals* (palm-sized cymbals), and flutes with circus, clowns, elephants, camels, tigers, and props (like a unicycle) created a fantastic carnival of sounds and images. These excesses were antithetical to the assumed 'purity' of the classical arts. (One of the strangest fusions of costumes for me was the image of Chandralekha on a trapeze wearing a circus costume but with Bharatanatyam-style hair adorned with flowers).

Uday Shankar's influences were referenced in a brief shot that recreated the 'man and machine' scene. A more elaborate reference to *Kalpana* was the drum and dance sequence. In that famous scene, hundreds of female dancers stood on drums as the male dancers beat the drums. Hundreds of soldiers hidden inside the drums later sprang out in an astonishing visual melodrama. The drum and dance scene was a spectacle which re-oriented the intimate aesthetics of darshan or gaze between the audience and performers. The choreography needed to be viewed from a distance, emphasizing the use of long shots. The fusing of dance, choreography, and cinematography in *Chandralekha* created a dimension for screen dances that no longer primarily abided by the emotional intimacy of rasa aesthetics. The packaging of the drama, action (sword fights), thrills (circus sequences), orchestral music, and dance created a new dimension of entertainment in Bombay films.

One only needs to contrast the visual aesthetics of both *Kalpana* and *Chandralekha* with *Shakuntala* (Figure 3.4) made by V. Shantaram shortly before, in 1943.

FIGURE 3.4   Poster for *Shakuntala*
Courtesy: NFAI, Pune.

Based on Kalidasa's famous Sanskrit drama, *Shakuntala* uses classical dance drama aesthetics to evoke moods of sringara (erotic desire) and *viraha* (separation, sorrow) through music, dance, and poetry. Set in a lush pastoral landscape resembling the mythic forest of Vrindavan (*tapavan* in Kalidasa's text), Shakuntala, played by the newcomer Jayashree, dallied with her playmates, not unlike the mythical Radha. The forest filled with birds (peacock, myna, and parrot) and animals (deer) and an undulating river were beautifully captured in the song *Man Ki Naiyya* (the mind's boat). The women in this bucolic landscape were integrated with nature. The music director Vasant Desai and the choreographer Prof. More created a pastoral utopia. Although limited in terms of the technological innovations that marked the later *Kalpana* and *Chandralekha*, the story of *Shakuntala* was poetically etched through the song and dance sequences. The film is also believed to be the first to have a 'wet sari' scene, that later became ubiquitous in Bombay films. *Shakuntala* was very successful in India and it was the first Indian film to be released in the west, but failed there.

The film *Rajnarthaki* (court dancer, 1941) which preceded *Shakuntala* also had a female dancer as protagonist. It was directed by Madhu Bose, a theatre personality and starred his wife Sadhana Bose, a well-known classical dancer. *Rajnarthaki* was made in Bengali, English, and Hindi and was released in the United States and distributed by Columbia Pictures. The dancing was entirely composed in the Manipuri style from eastern India and the classical musician Timirbaran Bhattacharya created the music. There were many other films around this time that were preoccupied with the courtesan genre with a female dancer as the protagonist, such as *Narthaki* (1940), *Chitralekha* (1941), among others, a trend that has continued until today.

A Bombay film that was saturated with spectacular song and dance sequences and was a mega-hit was *Jhanak Jhanak Payal Baje* (1955 [Figure 3.5]), directed by V. Shantaram.

Figure 3.5   Still from *Jhanak Jhanak Payal Baje*
Courtesy: NFAI, Pune.

It was shot in Technicolor and starred Kathak exponent Gopi Krishna and director Shantaram's dancer-wife Sandhya. The story was based on two people who were in love with each other and the classical arts. The choreography by Gopi Krishna mostly drew on the traditional Kathak repertoire. Vasant Desai composed the music and the lyrics were by poet Hasrat Jaipuri. Shantaram highlighted the *tandava* aspect of Gopi Krishna's dancing—with energetic leaps, fantastically paced footwork, and lightning spins—to create the melodrama of *Jhanak Jhanak Payal Baje*.

Gopi Krishna was born into a family of Kathak dancers; his sister was the famous Kathak dancer Sitara Devi, who was also a dancer in Bombay films. In one sequence in *Jhanak Jhanak Payal Baje*, based on Radha-Krishna *chherchhar* (amorous play connected to the Kathak repertoire) Kathak *bols* (mnemonic syllables), and *kavits* (poetry), *gopinis* (Radha's mates/the cowherd girls) were shown in a 'divine dance'. Gopi Krishna was even painted blue to look like Krishna. The scene evoked the sensibility of the folk tradition of *raslila*. However, there were other song and dance sequences such as *Nain Se Nain Nahi Milao* (Don't gaze into my eyes) in which the choreography followed modern aesthetics pioneered by Uday Shankar in *Kalpana*.

The innovative song and dance sequences in Bombay films such as *Jhanak Jhanak Payal Baje* and *Chandralekha* generated public interest in the classical dances during the 1940s and 1950s, just as Uday Shankar had hoped for with *Kalpana*. During this time, the song and dance sequences drew from Indian classical and folk dances and music to create innovative musical compositions and dance choreography. The studios in Bombay and Calcutta were associated with producing an indigenous kind of music and dance aesthetics. The films discussed so far charted a national imagery of classical beauty, mythic love, and idealized landscape. In the words of Christopher Pinney (1997: 834–67), they evoked 'a more "subliminal" and more "innocent" depictions of an idealized nationspace'. One could argue that is was a national space awash in tradition and culture.

On the other hand, the movies by Wadia Movietone such as *Diamond Queen* (Figure 3.6) etched a different nationalist image.

FIGURE 3.6 Still from *Diamond Queen*
Courtesy: NFAI, Pune.

The film departed from essentialist ideas of a national tradition to a more inclusive and hybrid model of Indian modernity. The heroine came to be known as 'Fearless Nadia'. She embodied the national space of fluid boundaries and transnational identities (an important aspect of Bollywood today). Rosie Thomas (2005: 66) observes:

> The Nadia persona—in all its complexity—is a figure at play within a liminal zone of fluid, racial, ethnic, gender and religious categories, where multiplicity and heterogeneity are celebrated. In the Wadia's stunt films the key players explore new identities through mimicry and impersonation, 'fixed' only temporarily to help disguise the inherent ginstabilities of the border and the anxieties about what within mainstream nationalism, is being repressed.

Nadia was trained in ballet. She was from Australia (but of Greek ethnicity) and was originally named Mary Evans. She became the most famous stuntwoman in Bombay films. Thomas identified her popularity with the *virangana* (female warrior model) of Sanskrit plays, who challenged the masculinity of males. Madhurika, the heroine in *Diamond Queen* was a Bombaywali (a resident of Bombay) and represented a cosmopolitan Indian identity that could negotiate and embrace 'otherness' (Thomas 2005: 35–69).

Helen, another Bombay film actress of foreign descent (Anglo-Burmese, in this case) was an iconic dance figure of cosmopolitanism. Although she was the anti-heroine or promiscuous dancer-vamp in most films, she was Bollywood's original 'item girl' (to be discussed later). Her famous dance in the film *Howrah Bridge* (1958), 'Mera Naam Chinchinchu' (My name is Chinchinchu) was a landmark sequence of imagining a transnational national space. The setting was a café in Calcutta, which, during the late colonial period, was an international node for people from Burma, China, England, and India. The choreography was a medley of different western dances, especially from the Swing era in America. The backup dancers executed with ease the usual partnering and steps associated with Swing. The choreography was by Surya Kumar, who belonged to a group of choreographers in Bombay equally adept at both Indian dance and western ballroom styles. Jay Borade, the choreographer of the film *Hum Apke Hain Kaun?* (Who Am I to You? 1994, which I discuss later) worked as Kumar's assistant for a long time.

Another significant example of a western cosmopolitan medley of shake and shimmy was in *Teesri Manzil* (1966). The film was a hit and launched the career of music director and composer Rahul Dev Burman. The song and dance sequences, inspired by Swing and Big Band music popular in the U.S. during that time, created a new trend in music and choreography. In the sequence *O Hasina Zulfowali* (O beautiful woman with tresses), Helen (she is of Anglo-Burmese origin) appeared as both a blonde and a brunette. The staging in a nightclub with elaborate sets had a sign that said 'Rocky' in the backdrop. The wide range of special effects included one where Helen emerged from inside a poster of a human eye. The choreography was by Herman Benjamin, who introduced the Shake, the Shimmy, and the Twist to Bombay films. He also choreographed the song and dance sequence *Jan Pehchan Ho* (You are known to me) for the film *Gumnaam* (1965), which was picked up by the Hollywood movie *Ghost World* (2001) for its opening credits and was featured in U.S. commercials for Heineken beer the same year. It is possible that 'Mera Naam Chinchinchu' of *Howrah Bridge* inspired the Swing dancing in 'Jan Pehchan Ho'. The interesting questions of media circulation of Bombay films, its reception in North America, and reme-diation associated with Jan Pehchan Ho have been analysed by Novack (2010). Overall, one could argue that the films of this period, especially the song and dance sequences, depicted a dialogue between national and international music and dance practices, technologies, and visual cultures; but they were significantly different from the globally oriented Bollywood song and dance sequences of today.

The aesthetics of *Mughal-E-Azam* (1960 [Figure 3.7]) or *Guide* (1965 [Figures 3.8 and 3.9]) were in direct contrast to the cosmopolitanism explored in films such as *Teesri Manzil* or *Howrah Bridge*. The song and

FIGURE 3.7   Still from *Mughal-E-Azam*
Courtesy: NFAI, Pune.

FIGURE 3.8   Poster for *Guide*
Courtesy: NFAI, Pune.

FIGURE 3.9   Still from *Pakeezah*
Courtesy: NFAI, Pune.

dance sequences in *Teesri Manzil* were heavily influenced by rock and roll music whereas both *Guide* and *Mughal-E-Azam* drew on syncretic Indian musical traditions (associated with an Indo-Islamic composite culture). *Mughal E-Azam* was based on the story of the Mughal prince Jahangir and his love for the court dancer and courtesan Anarkali. The classical/romantic aesthetic of the song and dance sequences of *Mughal-E-Azam* was created by the Kathak gurus Shambhu Maharaj and Lachchu Maharaj (of Lucknow *gharana*/school/style) and Gopi Krishna of *Jhanak Jhanak* fame. The music drew on north Indian classical genres. The lyrics were by the poet Shakeel Badayuni and the language in the songs was a mix of Urdu, Hindi, and Brajbhasha (a Hindi dialect spoken in north-central India). One of the famous song and dance sequences from the film, 'Mohe Panghat Pe Nandalal Ched Gayo Re' (On my journey to the river, Nandalal [Krishna] teases me), was rendered as a traditional *thumri* (a song style from the north Indian classical genre, often on the theme of the dalliances of Radha and Krishna), which is integral to Kathak dance. This song has deep roots in north India's courtly and courtesan music. It has been recorded by Indubala, who was a baiji trained by the famous Gauhar Jaan. These song and dance sequences have become classics, known for their grandeur, detailed stagecraft, sets, costumes, and cinematography. A flamboyantly colourized version of *Mughal-E-Azam* was released in 2004.

'Panghat Pe Nandalal' was set as a *mehfil* (gathering) in the court. Before the thumri began, Mughal emperor Akbar was shown praying in front of the Hindu deity Krishna, marking his religious pluralism. In the thumri, Anarkali, played by Madhubala, was imagined as Radha. The choreography resembled traditional Kathak chherchhar with elaborate sets and many backup dancers. In the song, Radha goes to fetch water from the river Yamuna with her clay pot where Krishna teases her and breaks her pot full of water by throwing a stone (a common story in the Kathak dance repertoire). In Kathak parlance, dancing to this kind of song is called *panghat lila* (a divine dance signified by the pot). The backup dancers in the scene were imagined as the *gopinis* (cowherd girls and Radha's playmates). They were resplendent in their beautiful costumes dancing in ensemble formations as well as sitting and playing sitar by water fountains. Radha's main dance motif was the *ghungat* (veil), again a typical Kathak motif that also marked her as a Hindu woman.

This identity of Anarkali as Radha was a contrast to her identity as a courtesan in the same film, which she embraced in the song and dance sequence 'Pyar Kiya To Darna Kya' (To Love Is Not to Fear). The male vocalist in the song was the north Indian classical maestro Ustad Bade Ghulam Ali Khan who sang a *tarana* (again from the north Indian classical dance and music genre). Here Anarkali was portrayed as a courtesan dressed in a Kathak outfit complete with headgear in the Islamic style. The gilded and ostentatiously decorated court was in sharp contrast to the muted green translucent fabric of Madhubala's costume. The *zardozi* (embroidery) on the costume was created by tailors from Surat and a goldsmith from Hyderabad designed the jewelry. The song was filmed in a set built as a replica of the Sheesh Mahal in Lahore Fort. One stunning aspect of the set was the presence of numerous small mirrors of Belgian glass, which were designed and crafted by workers from Firozabad in Pakistan. The mirrors multiplied the dancer's twirling image and created a dazzling panorama of images. The lighting of the set supposedly involved headlights from 500 trucks to create the dramatically multiplied image effect (https://en.wikipedia.org/wiki/Mughal-e-Azam).

The use of elaborate sets in films such as *Mughal-E-Azam*, *Jhanak Jhanak*, and *Chandralekha* is an aspect of Bombay film tradition inherited from Indian theatrical practices that is still going strong and being added to by digital graphics. Many 'item numbers' in Bollywood films now use special effects with digital media at least as much as they do elaborate sets. In this respect, Akbar Khan gives the example of the Hollywood film *Gladiator* where part of the set (such as the stadium, the famous Coliseum in Rome) was part manually built and part created through digital computer graphics. It was difficult if not impossible to distinguish between the real and the virtual (*Indian Express* 2011: July 17). Many contemporary Bollywood filmmakers continue to build sets to create special effects and splendor on screen, especially for the song and dance sequences, such as directors Sanjay Lila Bhansali (maker of *Devdas*, 2002), Ashutosh Gowarikar (*Lagaan*, 2001), and Sooraj Barjatya (whose set for the movie *Vivah* I visited and describe in the next chapter). And the courtesan film tradition has continued, with notable examples like *Pakeezah* (1972), *Umrao Jaan* (1981), and *Devdas* (2002), among many others. In other words, some of the key features of *Mughal-E-Azam* seem to be eternal in the Hindi movie industry; the grand sets and tragic courtesans never grow old.

Guide (1965), considered another classic in the film industry, was also a story about love and loss for the daughter of a courtesan, who had gained respectability by marriage to a rich archaeologist. The film was an Indo-American co-production and was simultaneously shot in Hindi and English. The song and dance sequences in the film had elaborate sets and Sachin Dev Burman composed the music. Choreographed by Fali Mistry and performed by Waheeda Rehman, the song and dance sequences in the film presented a new dance aesthetics that blended Kathak, Bharatanatyam, folk and freestyle dancing. This new hybrid aesthetics became a hallmark of Bombay 'filmy naach' before it was branded Bollywood. The sense of freedom and exuberance often associated with the term 'masti' (derived from *mast*, a Persian word associated with exuberant feelings of joy found in Sufi Qawwalis or Punjabi folks traditions such as Bhangra) is a quintessential emotion/affect of 'filmi naach'. It is palpably present in the song and dance sequence 'Katon Se Kheech Ke Ye Anchaal' (My Veil Has Been Snatched By Thorns). This is a scene where the heroine Rosie breaks free of her husband's repression, described in the lines: 'Keeping with her dangerous new desires ... riding in a cart and breaking a pot, thereby metaphorically breaking all conventions.' (Raheja 2002: quoted in http://www.rediff. com/entertai/2002/apr/18dinesh.htm).

Several song and dance sequences in the film were presented on an urban modern concert stage, no longer bounded by the courtly milieu. The picturization of 'Mose Chal kiye Jaye' (I have been duped) based on the common Krishna Radha theme (prevalent in the thumri style) was choreographed with eclectic sets of sculptures and fishnets. The backup dancers in the choreography were integrated with the cinematography in novel ways. They formed different clusters of moving bodies that were not the typical choreographic ensemble arrangements in Bombay films of circles and straight lines. The camera angles were also varied with long shots and close-ups that seamlessly blended with the choreography. The dancing was a fusion of movements from Bharatanatyam and Kathak.

The striking stage sets that accompany the song and dance sequence 'Piya To Se Naina Lage Re' (My Gaze Is Locked With My Lover) mapped the different stages of Rosie's success as a professional dancer. Beginning from a simple theatrical setting in a rural environment, the staging became grander and more ostentatious. The costumes, picturization, and dancing were based on the diverse folk dance traditions of India. The visualization of the choreography also marked the different festival seasons in India from Holi (festival of colors) to Diwali (festival of lights). Each stanza of the song unfolded a different choreography, costume, music, and setting. The innovative cinematography showed the backup dancers in novel ways. First, the camera only caught their moving feet but then their bodies filled the stage in various visual designs. The camera shots from the 'bird's eye position' (a common position for much choreography in Bombay films) had different perspectives. The sheer grace and beauty of Waheeda Rehman's dancing, her economy of movements, restraint, and energy made the scenes memorable.

The film *Pakeezah* (1972) by director Kamal Amrohi was another sensory feast. It evoked the splendor of Islamic courtly culture, much like *Mughal-E-Azam*. The story line, as in many Bombay films through the decades, was about a dancing girl, the daughter of a courtesan (*tawaif*), and her romance and separation. The song and dance sequences in this movie were based on north Indian classical music and Kathak dance. The music by Ghulam Muhammad and Naushad and lyrics by Kaifi Azmi and Majrooh Sultanpuri are classics, as is the choreography by Lucknow *gharana* Kathak legend Lachchu Maharaj. The song and dance sequence 'Inhi Logo Ne Le Liya Dupatta Mera' (These People Have Taken by Dupatta/Veil/Covering) was set in Amrohi's imagination of a *tawaif haveli* (courtesan quarter) in Lucknow. The open balconies, the arched doors and windows, the pillars, and the music and dance at once evoked a sense of place. The courtesan, Sahibjaan, played by Meena Kumari, danced in a *mujra* (Kathak soiree) for her clients who were seated around her. The scene also captured the backup dancers performing in the surrounding balconies, creating a wonderful visual depth with the camera angles. Meena Kumari slowly rose from a seated position with her wide skirt swirling and rising around her. She wore a red traditional Kathak outfit, with traditional jewelry such as the *jhapta / tasha* that rested on one side of her head. The sound of the *ghungroo*s (bells) around her ankle, footwork, *tabla* beats, swift movements, twirls, and delicate facial expressions created an aura of authentic beauty and intangible memory. The hundreds of bells worn around the ankle to accentuate the rhythmic beats in Kathak dance worked as the metaphor for the film as Sumita Chakravarty (1993: 293) describes: 'the feet become a motif throughout the film and are invested with layers of meaning ... Pakeezah, in the climactic scene of the film, dances on broken glass [to] show her defiance of aristocratic norms and values.'

The film *Umrao Jaan* made almost a decade later and directed by Muzzaffar Ali was based on the life of a famous Lucknow courtesan, based on the same theme. The aura of the Islamic court and the music and dance that went with it were carefully etched like a classical painting. In the song and dance sequence 'Dil Cheez Kya Hai' (This Thing Called Heart), Rekha in a red Kathak outfit was shown in a seated position in a mujra (Kathak soiree), which echoed a similar scene in *Pakeezah*. In *Umrao Jaan*, the mudras (hand gestures), *kalai* (wrists), and darting eyes of Kathak dance performed by Rekha were precise and subtle. The camera closed in to capture the intricacies of her facial expressions. The choreography by master Kathak dancer and choreographer Kumudini Lakhia was delightful to watch for its restrained sensibilities.

The importance of the song and dance sequence as the true identity of Hindi films is underlined by Lata Khubchandani (2004):

As music, melody, and dance took charge of listener's senses, every conceivable situation was right for a song. Besides clubs and cabaret numbers the *mujra* and *qawwalis* gained popularity. The dominance of the *tawaif* as a key character was perhaps also conceived as means of ensuring the centrality of song and dance. Outstanding perhaps have been *Pakeezah* and *Umrao Jaan*.

In her analysis of Bombay films, Sumita Chakravarty showed how the genre of courtesan films helped construct the narratives of Indian culture and gender identity. The picturization of the dance soirées in Bombay films with the chandeliers, water fountains, and arched doorways were interwoven with the sounds of tinkling bells, Urdu poetry, and classical and folk melodies accompanied by instruments like *sarangi*, *tabla*, and *sitar*. Together they constructed a particular sensibility of Indianness. In these and earlier Hindi films (including courtesan films), the song and dance sequences were integrated with the film's narrative. The sequences created a 'structure of feeling' that became identified with attributes of tradition and nation (albeit there were departures oriented more to western cosmopolitanism). Gopal and Moorti (2011: 22) argue that the films that evoked a sense of tradition and nation created a 'community of sentiments' that was both Indian and vernacular. I would add that it was largely through the song and dance sequences that these 'communities of sentiments' and the people inhabiting them were imagined as Indian.

In the 1970s and 1980s, the song and dance sequences in Bombay films were gradually dissociated from the narrative of the film. The action film genre used the song and dance sequences as distractions, yielding a different 'cinema of interruption' (Gopalan 2002). These were also the years when disco music, popularized by music director Bappi Lahiri, and disco dancing, popularized by actors Mithun Chakraborty and Rishi Kapoor, came to dominate the song and dance sequences. In the disco genre, the lyrics became unimportant and orchestration and fusion with western music emerged as the key to a new kind of urban cosmopolitanism.

The song and dance sequence 'I am a Disco Dancer' represented this new global modernity in a discotheque with psychedelic lighting and gyrating bodies.

A huge audience cheered as Mithun Chakraborty danced, shouted, and spelled 'D-I-S-C-O' and the sound reverberated across the audience. The backup dancers were like chorus musicians playing orchestral music in a line dance ensemble like the one made popular by *Saturday Night Fever* (1977) starring the dance sensation, John Travolta. Compared to such scenes today (which are common) the lighting and stage design were modest. Similar scenes and settings that preceded *Disco Dancer* (1982 [Figure 3.10]) were in the film *Hum Kissi Se Kum Nahi* (I Am No Less than Anyone, 1977). The jazzy upbeat music of the film was created by Rahul Dev Burman, an extraordinary composer who created enduring melodies that ranged from light classical and folk to fusion. The dancing in the film had stylized walks and everyday moves, elegantly executed by actor Rishi Kapoor. In both films, the

FIGURE 3.10   Poster for *Disco Dancer*
Courtesy: NFAI, Pune.

choreography was by Suresh Bhatt, who began in films as an assistant to Satyanarayan, a legendary choreographer of Bombay films, after whom the popular Satyam Dance Studio in Juhu, Mumbai is named. The studio is now used for rehearsals for backup dancers and reality show participants. The disco trend continued with actors Sridevi, Jitendra, and others who popularized the pelvic thrusts that came to be associated with the style. Sen (2008: 99) summarizes the Jazz and disco-inspired music of Bombay films that were integral to the dance of this period:

> The work of two 'untrained' musicians would usher in a new age of Indian popular music. The Kishore-RD sound with its multicultural influences, its frenetic pacing, its youthful upbeat rhythms—represented a complete rupture with the music of the 'golden age'. By the 70's disco had replaced rock as the cutting edge of international sounds.

The song and dance sequence that made choreography central to a film's path to commercial success was in *Tezaab* (1987 [Figure 3.11]).

FIGURE 3.11   Still from *Tezaab*
Courtesy: NFAI, Pune.

The number 'Ek Do Teen' (One Two Three) starring Madhuri Dixit was a super hit. The dance was choreographed by Saroj Khan, who was the first female dance choreographer to attain the status of male chore-ographers (*masterjis*) in Bombay films. The Filmfare best choreography award was invented for this film. 'Ek Do Teen' opened with Madhuri Dixit dancing a folksy number with her usual *jhatkas* (hip movements) and *matkas* (breast undulations that are the signature moves of cho-reographer Saroj Khan), a highly energetic *filmy naach* replete with *masti* (fun). The dancing also highlighted mobile and humorous facial expressions that included eye and brow movements and lip twitches. The folksy dancing at the beginning later changed to Hip-Hop inspired moves and the costume changed from skirts to pants. The backup danc-ers swelled in number as the dancing moved from one spot to another on a stage that looked like a ramp, the center of which was occupied by a giant gramophone. The dancing in 'Ek Do Teen' dissolved the differ-ence between vamp and heroine as the probing camera movement and shots enticed the audience to focus their attention on limbs, midriffs and breasts, highlighting the modes of shooting/voyeurism reserved earlier for vamps (Iyer 2014).

The choreography in 'Ek do Teen' was similar to another by Saroj Khan that became a huge hit. The dancer was Sridevi and the film was *Mr. India* (1987). Both Madhuri Dixit and Sridevi became known as the dancing divas of Bollywood and some of their typical moves such as jhatkas became codified as Bollywood dance moves. It is to be noted that Bollywood dance and its choreographers now were increasingly recognized as new and important, and some of the moves, like jhatkas, were taught in classes (Shreshtova 2011; Roy 2010). I will discuss more on this later.

Madhuri Dixit appeared as a sexy dancing girl again in *Khalnayak* (1993). The song and dance sequence 'Choli Ke Peechhe Kya Hai?' (What Lies Behind That Bodice?) was both daring and aesthetically striking (Sherril fuelled a censorship controversy). The dancers were all dressed in Rajasthani costumes of vivid earth tones. The visual design was MTV-like. In one section, the screen split into longitudinal sections to focus on the face and the eyes. The lyrics of the song were controversial for being sexually explicit. So were the heaving breasts that objectified the bodies of the dancers on the screen. The song and dance sequences such as this prepared the ground for 'item numbers' in mujra style that no longer had a connection to the past courtly flavors of restrain or eroticism. Shuddhabrata Sengupta (2005: 132) discusses the ability of numbers like 'Choli Ke Peechhe Kya Hai?' to function as 'vehicles of desire'. He explains the rising importance of cinematographers like Ashoka Mehta who created the glamorous look for 'Choli Ke Peechhe Kya Hai?' (Sengupta 2005: 134):

> It would not be incorrect to say that the 'song and dance sequence' is one space within the body of the Hindi film where the cinematographer gets to call the shots. The lavish costumes, the increasingly exotic locales and the presence of a huge production infrastructure make the song sequences the cinematographer's special domain—a space where he knows dazzle is called for.

Dance talents like Madhuri Dixit established firmly the era of 'item girls' and 'item numbers' in Hindi films. The idea of the heroine as the dancing girl who is explicitly sexualized and on display clearly broke from past representations of the heroine as chaste and virginal (even when they were courtesans). The heroine moved closer to the vamp.

Mixing Bhavas to Remix

A blockbuster film *Hum Apke Hain Kaun?* (HAHK) (Figure 3.12), with 14 song and dance sequences and lavish costumes and sets, is credited with creating a new standard for song and dance sequences in Bollywood films.

FIGURE 3.12   Still from *Hum Apke Hain Kaun?*
Courtesy: NFAI, Pune.

The film was directed by Sooraj Barjatya of Rajshri Productions, a prominent production house in Bollywood. The global prominence of Bollywood films, as well as the transformation from Bombay to Bollywood arguably began with this film. It played in theatres for almost a year and grossed more than $30 million, a remarkable take at the time. *Hum Apke Hain Kaun?* was choreographed by Jay Borade, who was trained in both western and Indian classical dances (and had been an assistant to Surya Kumar, mentioned earlier). The team of Sooraj Barjatya and Jay Borade also directed and choreographed the film *Vivah*, which I will discuss in the next chapter.

The dancing and choreography in HAHK threw together an eclectic fusion of western and Indian forms derived from the Punjabi folk dance bhangra but with a distinct Bollywood flavour. The movie celebrated the 'ideal' Indian family and traditional family values with wedding extravaganzas at the centre. It claims to be the first Bollywood film to run in mainstream cinemas in the U.S., U.K., and other parts of the world and arguably paved the path for other commercial Bollywood films in overseas markets. In these follower films, the song and dance sequences were created with an eye to the box office and overseas market rather a storyline' or script. Films such as *Dilwale Dulhania Le Jayenge* and *Dil To Pagal Hai* became hugely successful following the HAHK commercial model. Sudhanva Deshpande (2005: 197) writes that the 'HAHK' formula was picked up with lightning speed by the industry. He (2005: 201) describes HAHK in terms of the 'desires of unbridled consumerism, ritualism, and religiosity through the fantasy of the contradiction—free Hindu undivided family, became a massive blockbuster.' Deshpande (2005: 194) points out that 'the rural and urban laboring classes also disappear in the current trend of song and dance picturization. They were replaced by rich, slick and candy faced heroes and model like westernized heroines [exception is Lagan].' Despite that, or perhaps because of it, Bollywood now established itself as a major entertainment industry at the global scale.

Song and dance sequences picturized in exotic locales with superb cinematography began to claim a life separate from the actual film, such as the number 'Chhaiya Chhaiya' from the film *Dil Se* (From The Heart). This number brought the concept of the 'item girl' to the forefront. The dancing on top of a moving train in 'Chhaiya Chhaiya', surrounded by nature (located who knows where; Assam? Himachal? The Western Ghats?), as well as the Rajasthani costumes, the Rajasthani folk-inspired dancing, and the catchy music by A.R. Rahman, made the sequence memorable. The lyrics by Gulzar were based on a traditional Sufi song by Bulleh Shah. The visualization of the music was so compelling that it wedded the cinematography indelibly to the song and helped create a new visual music genre. 'Chhaiya Chhaiya' marked the arrival of the Indian music video with a particular jerky camera work, rapid editing technique, vivid colors, and high-end, digitally produced images. It also identified A.R. Rahman as the leader in ushering in a new kind of contemporary Indian musical composition. The choreography by Farah Khan also put her on the map and she won the Filmfare best choreographer award for the film. The music video of 'Chhaiya Chhaiya' became a global hit. It was later used during the opening credits of the Hollywood film *Inside Man* (2006), starring Denzel Washington and Jodie Foster. These sequences now produced Indianness through Punjabi bhangra rather than classical Indian forms (Rao 2010). The film created a new ethos of consumerism in Bollywood films where modernity was no longer associated with urbanism as in the disco phase. 'Chhaiya Chhaiya' showed that Bollywood dance and choreography had gained a new status and identity in the capitalist market of global pop and urban culture.

Shuddhabrata Sengupta (2005: 118) observes that 'a new aesthetic filtered via the music television entered Hindi cinema in the early to mid-nineties'. The song and dance sequences that were depicted in exotic locales with hi-tech cinematography claimed an existence that was separate from the actual film. The interdependent relationship between Bollywood song and dance sequences and the music video market established a new global/market niche for Bollywood industry. The remixing of traditional or old Bombay film music in new packages began gaining popularity. Its spread was propelled by 'remix' hits like the controversial video 'Kata Laga' by DJ Doll. The video created a controversy about censorship and women's sexuality, not unlike the song and dance sequence of 'Choli Ke Peechhe Kya Hai' in the film *Khalnayak*.

The idea of 'remix', which is not confined to music videos but also in the use of language, such as the mix of Hindi and English (Hinglish), ushered in a new urban cultural phenomenon in the Indian diaspora (Vishnu 2003). The trendy pop 'remix' genre celebrated the simultaneity of being South Asian and international in cities like London and Birmingham (Couglan 2009). The popularity of the 'remix' videos showed that the 'item number' was going to be the driver of Bollywood films in the twenty-first century. The 'item numbers' were now generally danced by 'item girls' who were no longer the vamps of past Bombay films, but were often the main female protagonist or some glamorous and established film star who appeared as a guest performer. The success of the 'item girl' led to the creation of the 'item boy' in films such as *Desi Boyz* (2011) and *Garam Masala* (2005). Although the term was not yet in circulation, the original 'item boy' was dancer-actor and choreographer Prabhu Deva who created some memorable song and dance sequences in the 1990s.

The 'item number' in Bollywood films came to function like music videos with eclectic styles of dancing and music but packaged with a particular 'remix' aesthetics associated with commodities, advertising, and cosmopolitanism. They now had a life of their own. They were released many months before the film was released. They appeared on television programs and circulated on video, cable, DVD, and the internet. In fact, the popularity of a song and dance sequence now determined the box office success of the film. Anustup Basu (2008: 153–76) contends that the song and dance sequences operate like 'designer products that can invoke bodies, spaces, and objects that can arrive from any visual universe'. The primary thrust was to produce arresting visuals that juxtaposed a variety of sexual, exotic, and rapidly moving images. This popularity of 'remix' videos was identified early in the Indian English newspaper *the Hindu* by Vishnu (6 August 2003):

It is no big deal anymore, that remix albums are selling like hot cakes. A few months ago, Indipop saw a renaissance in the remix scene, which started by a song by DJ Aqueel called Tu Hai Wohi, Kaliyon Ka Chaman by Shaswati, Kaanta Laga by DJ Doll and many more followed—and today, it has become some sort of a rule that every music company must release a remix album, featuring a video where three or four skimpy clad models gyrate to gravity defying pelvic moves!

The song and dance sequences and their choreography in Bollywood films were now designer products that did not belong to any single nation or location but were transnational and hybrid products of postmodernism. This postmodern hybridity was writ large on the canvas of films like *Dhoom 2*. The hi-tech thriller was a mega-hit sequel to the mega-hit *Dhoom*. There was also a *Dhoom 3* (and *Dhoom 4* is in pre-production), marking the rhizomatic franchise production of the Dhoom series. *Dhoom 2* was an extraordinary visual extravaganza that set new Bollywood standards. This cop-and-robber film starred Hrithik Roshan, Aishwarya Rai, Abhishek Bachchan, and Bipasa Basu. The story spanned several continents, from Africa to Asia to South America. Hrithik Roshan was an international thief who planned to steal a priceless artifact in Bombay. Aishwarya Rai was a wannabe master thief who fell for Hrithik. This was the basic story line, with the cop (Abhishek Bachchan) always being outwitted by the thief Hrithik. Both Hrithik and Aishwarya exuded the cosmopolitan aura of western fashion models with their perfect bodies, stylish accessories, tanned looks, and golden hair highlights. Hrithik sported Pepe jeans, drove Suzuki bikes, and was the quintessential American hero, whereas Ash, as she is popularly known, wore leather boots, micro miniskirts, and bikini tops, reminding us of MTV queen Britney Spears.

The song and dance sequence 'Dil Laga Na Dil Jala Se' (Attach Your Heart Or Else It Will Burn) opened in a Samba festival in Brazil. After a few images of acrobatic Capoeira leaps, the audience was confronted with the sculpted body and youthful exuberance of Hrithik. Displaying his narcissistic musculature, Hrithik glided, grinded, jumped, and swayed with ease and grace. Aishwarya, in a white miniskirt and bikini top, exhibited her slender body and bare legs more fearlessly than her male counterpart. The digital effects in the sequence were spliced with elaborate costumes of the carnival, creating a colourful montage. The screen kept moving from one image to another in rapidly edited shots creating a dizzying array of images. A techno-Indo-MTV 'remix'was produced that was neither bounded by geographical boundaries nor by any ethnic identity. Note that the lyrics of the song itself were in Hinglish. With its bold images (leather, metal, acrobatic bodies) and international brand endorsements, *Dhoom 2* delivered the promise of liberation from geographical boundaries and bounded aesthetics by creating a new 'remixed commodity aesthetics' of social aspiration. A liberation achieved through the luxurious aspirational emotion of looking Euro-American and maintaining a Euro-American lifestyle. *Dhoom 2* personified a new Indian membership in the transnational and free-floating world of commodity images that was both global and Indian.

The transnational identities in Bollywood film song and dance sequences create the desire to consume the images and goods of foreign brands and transform identities (much like the reality show makeover culture discussed in Chapter 2). The influences of the 'commodity aesthetics' circulated through Bollywood song and dance sequences are not confined to Bollywood dance, but also influence classical, folk, and contemporary avant-garde concert forms, where spectacularization and hyper-visualization dominate today. Even in the so-called *mujra* style sequences in Bollywood films such as 'Sheila Ki Jawani' (Sheila's Youth) from *Tees Maar Khan*, the movements no longer resemble any particular dance style or identifiable origin. The lyrics of the song (also in Hinglish) 'celebrated' the woman's body with explicit sexual language. The costume in the opening scene looks like a bikini version of something Indian but shifts to shirts and pants in later shots. As in *Dhoom 2*, the camerawork is jerky and choppy with frequent cuts that fragment limbs, breasts, and torsos and create a sensation of kinesthetic and visual disorientation. The 'item numbers' featuring an 'item girl' or 'item boy' are now independent products that are malleable and not attached to any ethnicity. They circulate in various media and exhibit new cosmopolitan gender codes of femininity and masculinity (more on this in Chapter 6).

In later chapters I show that the rise of dance reality shows in India is based on a complex intersection of lives, desires, aspirations, and experiences of dancers, choreographers, and spectators, and perhaps above all, the producers and marketers of Bollywood as a product. I also show that the celebrity culture of reality shows is intimately associated with the dancing of the 'item girl' and 'item boy' of Bollywood films. Bombay cinema/Bollywood has played an overwhelming role in shifting the aesthetics of desire from a tradition-inspired mythopoetic context to a new aesthetic of commodity and consumption. Expressed usually through narratives of romance heightened in song and dance sequences, representations of the erotic desire in Bombay films in the past had drawn mostly on Indian classical and folks dance forms. But now the classical dance aesthetics are mostly relics. Even western dances inspired by ballroom or disco appear retro, performed in the style of a pre-liberalized Indian filmi-naach lacking the gloss and brand of Bollywood. The hybrid dance fusions that dominate the songs and dances today are inspired by commodity aesthetics driven by a lifestyle of global consumption. The idea of desire in these sequences is no longer attached to some romantic notions of love, seduction, devotion, or mysticism, but with aspirations of consumption, brands, sex, and luxury. This aesthetic transition, driven by technology and the global reach of Bollywood (as market and source of raw material), is articulated through 'remix'. This idea is further explored in the next chapter with a focus on the training, making and on the various embodiments of dance.

4

Flexing and Remixing Bodies

In Mumbai, the autos are my lifeline for doing fieldwork in far-flung places. Crawling like fearless ants in traffic crammed with cars, trucks, and pedestrians, these autos are everywhere. In addition to the usual traffic hazards, last week I spotted a solitary elephant sauntering in the hullaballoo in Andheri; another time I saw one in Bandra. The thought of my auto squashed under a truck or an elephant's foot has not escaped my mind, but still it is better to be in an auto than a rented car in Mumbai. Parking is a worse nightmare. Despite the high ambient traffic noise, I see that every second person is chatting on his or her mobile phone. The heat and humidity that engulf Mumbai just before the arrival of the monsoons choke the streets with sweat, smoke, and dust. But they remain packed with pedestrians. Whether it is a quick chaat at the Hill Road Chaat Centre or an aimless browse through the roadside hawker shops, Mumbai is a city of shopkeepers and customers. The street kids are also active members of Mumbai's large informal economy—selling newspapers, books, magazines, bangles, and sundry cotton stuff. Every time my auto stops at a light, a beaming face greets me and thrusts a book or a magazine in my face. The innocent face of a ten-year-old boy cajoles me ... 'didi ye aap ke liye hai' (elder sister, this is for you). As if it is a gift for me. This is how I end up buying a new pulped book written by a young Indian-American just after she graduated from high school.[1] It still sits on my bookshelf and reminds me of the angelic face that negotiated with me to buy the piece of junk for Rs 250.

Such unrelenting survival instincts, infectious vitality, and indomitable aspirations are characteristics that the gritty streets of Mumbai share with the ruthlessly competitive world of Bollywood dance and dance reality shows. During my fieldwork in the dance halls of Mumbai, I encountered a world of unbridled aspirations filled with intense passion among young dancers. They expressed themselves through their outpourings of exaltations and disappointments. I was immersed in their world, even if for a short duration. I see a so-called version of this world on Indian satellite television all the time, a world filled with dreams and the glitter of celebrity culture. I wore my anthropological hat to explore the world that is not seen on screen: the dance classes, rehearsals, struggles, and dreams of young dancers and choreographers in India. I explored 'who they are, how they are being trained, what motivates them', how they experience their dance, as well as the behind-the-scene production process of image-making and choreographing for cinema and television.

However, before I report on what I saw and heard in the backstage of the industry it is useful to provide some background on how to approach this material. Implicit here is what I had discussed in Chapter 2 at length about consciousness and desire, where the former is embodied and the latter is aesthetic/emotive. Here I will further explore the aesthetic/emotive in the contemporary context as the aspirational emotion of 'remix (already touched upon in Chapter 3) through the

---

[1] Apparently, the book *How Opal Mehta Got Kissed, Got Wild, and Got a Life*, was plagiarized from several sources, taken off the shelves, and destroyed by the publisher.

framework of embodiment. Therefore, I begin by exploring the concept of 'embodiment' (as embodied subjectivity) and its connection to desire to examine how the dominant aesthetic emotion once associated with the song and dance sequences in films—rasa—is transformed not just through technological and aesthetic innovations on screen, but through the actual training of the body. I also explore how technology influences bodily knowledge transmission and how bodies adapt to technology. 'Remix', I have proposed in the previous chapter, expresses the new training techniques, film editing, and choreography of Indian screen dances. Since the older boundaries between high and low and classical and popular are being dissolved under globalization, a new emotion/affect associated with 'remix' is replacing the traditional codes and aesthetics of rasa (that was reinvented through the classical arts during nationalism). In order to explore Indian dance in this present condition, the phenomenological concept of 'embodiment' can offer us insights into how desires/aspirations are experienced and moulded through interactions with technology and the political economy of contemporary Indian culture.

As a dancer and an anthropologist I am excited to see the rising importance of the body as a locus of cultural analysis in social theory fora. Thomas Csordas (1994: 6) argues that 'this turn to the body in contemporary scholarship reflects the uneasy postmodern condition of indeterminacy. Body in social theory emerges as the "ground of culture"'. Needless to say, the dancing body is a powerful site for analysing cultural change.[2] I suggest that the intersection of the dancing body and the screen occupy a central place for studying the ongoing processes of subject formation and embodiment in contemporary Indian culture (more on this in Chapters 5 and 6). Many years ago Mauss (1934/1973:

[2] See Royona Mitra's (2015) recent work on Akram Khan on mobility, embodiment, and interculturalism in the UK.

1950) had noted this discomfiting subjective-objective grounding of the body, as it is at the same time the original tool with which humans shape their world and the original substance out of which the human world is shaped. Here I draw on overlapping traditions of ideas and practices in an eclectic and creative endeavour to examine the fundamental changes in the ways our bodies are experiencing culture and how culture is being shaped by our bodies.

The dancing body in Indian culture is an important site for analysing the perceptual changes taking place in our sensory world, affecting how we experience culture, self, and subjectivity. Thus, I propose that 'embodiment' of both *experience* and *expression* (see Chapter 1) offers a conceptual framework for analysing Indian dance as it transitions from a national narrative of tradition and culture associated with devotional and mystical desires to a market-driven panoply of 'item numbers'.

In the first section that follows, 'Embodiment of Devotional Desire to Commodity Desire', I briefly describe the traditional training system of gurushisya parampara that was adopted and adapted by the modern institutions of dance training in India and then link it to the changing aesthetics and contexts of screen dances. In the second section titled 'The Production of a Sequence', I move to Film City Studios to explore the processes of image making in the song and dance sequences in Bollywood films and the voices of choreographers as they reflect on their personal experiences of the commodification of aesthetics. In the third section, 'Dancing between Mumbai and Kolkata', I shift my focus to the training in dance halls in Mumbai and the dance classes and studios in Kolkata to analyse the pedagogical changes in training the body, especially among reality show participants and choreographers. I report on an audition for the hit reality show *Dance India Dance* held in Kolkata in 2012 to expand the context from classes to TV production and underline the interdependence of the film and TV worlds. My focus in these different ethnographic contexts—a movie set in Mumbai, classes in Mumbai and Kolkata, and a TV audition in Kolkata—is to highlight the overlapping worlds of Bollywood and dance reality shows and the construction of the new embodiments of desire/aspiration in diverse contexts, expressed through the aesthetics of 'remix'.

Scholars now agree that during nationalism (in the pre- and postcolonial phases) Indian identity was created through a particular (Sanskritic) narrative of tradition that drew on aesthetic emotion (the *bhava-rasa* structures of feeling), deep subjectivity, and a long civilizational lineage. Various dances were selectively deployed to construct a modern national identity (Chakravorty 1998; Coorlawala 2004; Meduri 1988; Soneji 2012; Walker 2014). A tradition was invented to serve modernity (Hobsbawm and Ranger 1983). These dances were based on a model of durable and reproducible practice inculcated through institutions such as guru, abhyas/riyaz, parampara, that created a habitus arising from a sense of continuity and tradition (I have analysed dance riyaz or practice in the context of 'habitus' in Chakravorty 2004).[3] However, this kind of embodiment achieved through a grounded and reproducible emotional patterning from deep immersion in a particular dance style has come unmoored due to the multiple economic and technological changes of the last two decades that have resulted in the explosion of consumer culture in India.

My larger objective is to understand the crisis and reconstitution of the habitus that once connected identities to territorial locations and has led to 'de-territorialization' (Arjun Appadurai's term, 1997). I show

---

[3] As Hobsbawm and Ranger (1983: 1) explain: '"Invented tradition" is taken to mean a set of practices, normally governed by overtly or tacitly accepted rules and of a ritual or symbolic nature, which seek to inculcate certain values and norms of behaviour by repetition, which automatically implies continuity with the past. In fact, where possible, they normally attempt to establish continuity with a suitable historic past.'

that Bollywood dance and dance reality shows are important sites for seeing the embodied/disembodied aesthetics of 'remix' that are producing new subjectivities and narratives of nationhood and cosmopolitanism in India. In short, a new habitus is brought into being through the 'remix' practices of dance today.[4]

But before we get to that, it may be helpful to get a clear understanding of the relevance of the term 'practice' to analyse 'embodiment' in the context of dance. I emphasize this because practice in Indian dance (especially in the classical styles) has deep meaning and is expressed through words such as 'riyaz' or 'abhyas'. These terms are also connected to pedagogical structures connecting guru or teacher and student or *shisya* (to be elaborated later). Thus, practice/praxis is an important analytical node in dance scholarship both in the west and the east as it refers to both social theory (or a body of ideas) and the corporeal actions of the body enacted through habits. Pierre Bourdieu's conceptualization of habitus, drawn from a phenomenological understanding of practice, has been important in movement scholarship (Farleigh 2000; Bender 2005). It enabled bodily meaning to be located outside discourses of representation, in the realm of experience and emotion (which connects 'embodiment' to the framework of experience and emotion as mentioned earlier). It integrated meaning with memory that was not nostalgia, but was embodied in a more immediate and tangible way. The concept of the habitus arising from durable and embedded systems of bodily comportments grounded particular bodies in particular places, which evoked specific aesthetic sensibilities and emotional patterns (Chakravorty 2004). In the context of Indian dance forms, the cultural rootedness of practice (however reconstructed, re-invented, or transnational) was embodied through a particular student-teacher

---

[4] See Born (2010) for a critique of habitus, also Berthoz (2000 mentioned in Foster 2011).

relationship based on gurushisya-parampara and the aesthetics of bhava and rasa (Vatsyayan 1977).

These particular embedded and reproducible forms of practice produced through a sense of emplacement and a long civilizational lineage are rapidly changing in contemporary India. A new form of dance practice is re-articulating and transforming the embodied aesthetics and ideology of Indian dances, where dancers inhabit multiple places and identities. This new practice is a 'remix', in which a fluid, porous, and ephemeral understanding replaces the notion of authentic, stable, and durable practice. In this new form of practice of mixing of forms—high and low, classical and folk, Indian and international—cultural forms mishmash to produce endless hybridity. 'Remix' is the postmodern experience of the consumption of pastiche where the lines between culture and commodity are blurred (Jameson 1991, 1998; Harvey 1989). 'Remix' recreates the intimate relationship between bodies and technology as well as the articulation of hybridity. The song and dance sequences in Bollywood as well as on reality shows capture this new global Indian modernity, perceptible through a new mediatized, technologized, and commercialized practice of dance. It is marked by the indeterminacy of the body in postmodernism, as it exists in a flux between the experiential 'subjective and objective continuum' posited by Csordas (2004). It captures the idea that in postmodern culture, realities are permeated and fragmented by technology so that the subjective and objective are diffused (discussed in Chapter 2 in the context of film reception, televisual culture, and the construction of the post-modern subject). I offer here such a dynamic and complex notion of the body and subjectivity.

In this new de-territorialized and mediatized embodiments, cultural and individual memories are unsettled due to media and migration (Appadurai 1995). The previous chapter charted such a trajectory for screen dances as they evolved from the mythopoetic/religio-aesthetic genres in Bombay films to 'item numbers'. In this chapter, I chart this trajectory as it has evolved from the everyday practice associated with riyaz and affect (derived from bhava-rasa/religio-aesthetic) to the consumption of images represented through 'remix'.

I begin from the training systems in classical Indian dance and explore how the embodied aesthetics imparted through that training was/is connected to *bhakti rasa* (devotional desire). I argue here that this kind of devotional and/or aesthetic desire that was foundational to Indian concert dances in the postcolonial period (supported by state institutions) is in radical flux. Now dancers learn different dance styles from different contexts and teachers to create flexible bodies and hybrid identities. The idea of flexible bodies has been discussed by Kedar (2014) in a diasporic context. The notion of bhakti rasa has been replaced by voluptuous desires and spectacular commodities. 'Remix' is the conceptual node that integrates the everyday practice of Indian dance with its emergent cultural habitus (although whether it can be called a habitus is debatable as notions of cultural memory and unconscious habits are in turbulence). It is both a method of dance practice and an aesthetic style or affect. Condensing the past meaning of riyaz and rasa into both experience and representation, 'remix' encapsulates a subjective and objective continuum of identity.

Embodiment of Devotional Desire to Commodity Desire

Training in classical Indian dances is primarily oral. The learning is a gradual process of enculturation in the dance heritage (through practices and routines). The aim is to perpetuate this knowledge from generation to generation by forging lifelong relationships. In classical dance, one's identity as a dancer is defined in part by the identity of one's teacher, who traces it back in line to a founding forefather (seldom female) who is traced back in genealogical terms to a known caste group. This is what perpetuates the social organization of gurushisya-parampara and civilizational lineage. In the past, this was not only an economic arrangement but was meant to preserve the very 'essence' of the art form as pristine and uncorrupted by outside influences. Since knowledge was transmitted orally, it was the student's duty to replicate the teachings through riyaz.[5] The student's aim was to embody the guru in every way and the latter's knowledge was immortalized through the student. This was a very personal relationship and studying with one guru for a long period created a special bond. It often required co-habitation and complete emotional, intellectual, spiritual, and physical surrender to one's guru. In return, the student became assimilated into the genealogical lineage of an unbroken tradition and became an authoritative representative of that particular style (Chakravorty 2008; Morelli 2010). This was the idealized notion of gurushisya-parampara.

Let us focus on the key concept of bhakti to explicate some of the shifts in the Indian dance experience. One of the primary emotions in the classical Indian dances is bhakti rasa. This means igniting intense devotion through dance. Bhakti requires a complete surrender of one's ego through loving devotion to god. In the dance-training model of gurushisya parampara, this kind of unconditional devotional love forms the core relationship between the student and the guru, where the latter becomes an equivalent of god (see Chakravorty 2005). The emotional engagement created through bhakti is connected to Indian aesthetic structures of feelings (the bhavas and rasas) which supposedly produce the yogic spiritual body (derived from the Upanishidic traditions discussed in Chapter 2) of the dancers. For instance, a student of classical dance begins from simple footwork and years later moves to complex patterns that are elaborated through fluid hand gestures,

---

[5] My intimate knowledge of Kathak dance came from a decades-long immersion in riyaz.

eye movements, and footwork. The movements are structured around mnemonic syllables played on percussions. The student learns to memorize and count the rhythms and infuse the movements with kinesthetic memory and emotion. She learns to express emotions of devotion and desire by dancing to songs from the classical musical genres. The experience of time in the *tala* structures is circular and continuous just as space is both internal and external. The spatial and temporal experiences emerge from repetitive kinesthetic explorations. They are simultaneously cosmological and real. During performance, space and time are moulded through a subjective experience of making anew. This phenomenological approach to space and time is what sets Indian dance apart from western choreographic conventions (that emerge from an objective-scientific time/space construct; see Foster (2011) regarding choreography and its origins). After independence, when the state, especially the central government, became the official (and primary) patron of culture, the model of gurushisya-parampara became an important ideological device for protecting, preserving, and promoting India's national heritage.

The ideology of parampara once fostered by state institutions and many teachers or gurus is undergoing significant changes in the current context as the experiences of bhakti and sringara are commodified due to the contraction of state institutions and their replacement by market relations. The classical dances are now global art forms with diverse practitioners and audiences in an increasingly transnational context.[6] As Indian dance is moulded by transnational flows of images, global networks, international practitioners and markets, the social organization

---

[6] This does not mean that the classical dances or Indian dancers were not transnational before, but the speed and depth of circulation is unprecedented. For a nuanced understanding of the transnational history of Indian dance, see Srinivasan (2012).

and practices of gurushisya-parampara are undergoing significant transformations. This new embodied aesthetics of Indian dance is no longer bounded by nation and tradition (propped up by state initiatives and dance festivals). Though I focus on new genres such as Bollywood dance and dance reality shows, it is necessary to recognize that even the classical forms are impacted by the practices and ideologies of 'remix'.[7]

My argument here is that some of these foundational concepts and structures of Indian dances are changing due to cultural shifts in a liberalized India, specifically pertaining to dance training, travel, and explosion of electronic media. Appadurai (1997: 44–5) observes this new condition of 'remix' and hybridity in another context when he writes:

> The sort of transgenerational stability of knowledge that was presupposed in most theories of enculturation (or, in slightly broader terms, socialization) can no longer be assumed .... As the shapes of cultures grow less bounded and tacit, more fluid and politicized, the work of cultural reproduction becomes a daily hazard. Far more could, and should, be said about the work of reproduction in an age of mechanical art.

Some of this cultural fluidity and change are played out in the microcosm of the aspiring halls of fame in Mumbai, where the tabla player, the musicians and the guru of a typical dance context have been replaced by DJs, big stereo systems, the choreographer and his/her assistant, and a schedule to keep track of the renters of the space. In these studios, the dancers and choreographers gather to learn, practice, and choreograph 'item numbers' that draw on a variety of movements from a variety of cultures. The cultural landscape of the dance halls in Mumbai or dance

---

[7] However, postmodern hybridity is by definition internally contradictory. Therefore, it is no surprise that there are also many examples—such as Kalakshetra and Nrityagram—of the classical dances being preserved though institutions that closely resemble the gurukul tradition that nonetheless operate within a global culture-industry.

studios in Kolkata reflects a new dance culture in India that is hybrid, porous, and a part of the transnational culture-industry.

Many dancers and choreographers in Bollywood spoke to me of the erosion of the cultural and aesthetic codes connected to the traditional methods of imparting knowledge of the body. Geeta Kapoor, who has some Bharatanatyam training, and was assistant to the eminent chore-ographer Farah Khan, and now is a judge on the hit reality show *Dance India Dance*, talked about the emergence of 'item numbers':

> In college people asked me to do fashion shows. I was partnered with dancer Javed Jaffrey. I worked with Ken Ghosh [a music video director, known for the hit musical *Ishq Vishk*]. I have done forty or so videos with him. I have been working with Farah Khan as her assistant from 1994. I have choreographed *Arman, Ashoka,* and *Pyar Me Kabhi.* I also do a lot of film shows and events. This is the time of the 'item numbers'. Dancers have specific looks and glamour, they are professionals. We know that dancing is all about having a good frame of mind and creating a good look.

The 'specific looks and glamour' Geeta Kapoor references here is associated with a certain kind of packaging associated with urbanism, professionalism, and a global Indian lifestyle. Pathak calls these new bodily dispositions and practices 'presentability' and it is an embodied form of cultural capital not unlike 'remix'. Pathak (2014: 322) writes that: 'Presentability—the expression of this global Indian identity at the site of the body—is rooted in the social position of the middle classes, specifically urban middle-class professionals, although it is consumed as an ideal by a wide range of Indians.' Presentability is about being groomed in a particular way which is encoded in the changing con-ception of an Indian body, its ability to wear western clothes, appear well-groomed with clear skin, and hair highlights and sport a consump-tion-oriented lifestyle. This ideology of presentability is related to the idea that cosmetically improved bodies provide a sense of happiness and control in reality shows (discussed in Chapter 2). Similarly, here the body itself is transformed into a sign, a certain kind of packaging of cosmopolitan hybrid inspired by the images represented in song and dance sequences of Bollywood films.

The older dancing body constructed through bhakti and the relationships it forged between teacher and student or god and devotee are no longer relevant to the inter-generational transmission of knowledge. The structures of feeling associated with bhava rasa appear on 'item numbers' as fleeting emotions, almost cartoons or caricatures, of a bygone era. These bodies are not embedded in any particular cultural style. They are instruments on which movements are crafted using 'copy and paste' techniques. Therefore, various movements are uprooted from specific contexts and remixed to produce an 'item number'. They reflect the commodity-oriented consumption practices of a global and urban Indian postmodernity. Geeta Kapoor says:

> We don't have formal dance training schools for Bollywood dances except for Shiamak Davar [although this is not true anymore]. Earlier, people got training in Bharatanatyam, Kathak, folk styles, etc. But you have to remember that earlier, dancers were fillers in Bombay films. Choreographers have given the dancers a presence in Bombay films. They make Rs 2,500–3,000 a day. We have a union. Now young people learn their moves in fashion shows. They also learn from music videos. Often their first encounter with dance is Bollywood dance numbers on television. They imitate them.

In Bollywood, the changes are not only encoded in the nature of dance practice once associated with traditional embodied aesthetics, but in the negotiations with new editing techniques, computer graphics, and an impetus to represent bodies that are inspired by commodity images. These sculpted dancing figures very often unite with fashion models, as fashion shows and film dance numbers unite to create a common platform to display commodities.[8]

The film dances that were once deemed frivolous and lowbrow by the educated middle classes in India (in comparison to the classical concert dances) are now regularly taught in dance schools along with the classical forms. The live staged performances of the film dances are a big draw in India and among the diaspora and it circulates now as authentic Indian identity (see David, 2010 for an exploration of Bollywood dance among the South Asian diaspora in the U.K.). The result, Shreshtova (2011) argues, has been a vital transformation of a medium called 'filmee dance' or dance choreographies from films, influenced by the then-prominent classical and folk performance traditions, to a medium called Bollywood dance which has, in turn, influenced performed expressions of Indianness. This constant movement of dance from one medium to another or from one cultural context to another has resulted in a coalescing of various dance genres into perpetual hybrid formations that produce novel identities.[9] The dance spaces I traversed during my fieldwork were part of this new discursive field of Indian dance of fluid borders and aspiring choreographers and dancers. They came from all walks of life, breaking down many previous notions of middle class respectability as they forge hybrid and novel identities (more on this in Chapter 6).

Producing a Sequence

On the sets of *Vivah* (2006; a film about the virtues of arranged marriage), in Film City Studios, the award-winning choreographer Jay Borade shared with me the new processes of commodification of images that are now part of the new Bollywood culture industry, to be distinguished

---

[8] The changing status of film dancers is reflected in how their title has changed from film extras to back-up dancers to junior artists.

[9] Weidman (2012) writes about this phenomenon in the context of music.

from the commercial industry of old Bombay films (see Figure 4.1). (I focus on the production of images to emphasize that the dancing in reality shows is a continuation of the same process of commodification of images that produces the mediatized embodiments of new camera work and editing technologies.) Borade explained how music videos and performance practices derived from western MTV aesthetics that explicitly sexualize the dancing body have been competing with the traditional/older romantic aesthetics of dance that informed the song and dance sequences of commercial Hindi cinema. This phenomenon, according to him, was transforming the industry.

I accompanied Sanjay Dabade, a renowned art director of Bollywood films, to the sets of *Vivah* in Goregaon (where Film City is located) where I met Jay Borade. Sanjay was designing the sets for *Vivah* (2006), a film by Rajshri Productions. The set included a terrace where the hero and heroine (played by Bollywood stars Shahid Kapoor and Amrita Rao) romance. The story was a family drama based on Indian values, I

FIGURE 4.1   Jay Borade and Author in Film City Studios, Mumbai
Source: Author.

was told. When I arrived at the set, there was chaos all around. There were about 40 to 50 people working on different parts of the set, constructing platforms at various levels. Putting the set together required detailed craftsmanship for work such as laying a tiled floor, which was the most intricate aspect of the set; it was built with small marble tiles/chips that had to be laid one at a time in a pattern of a floral design. The terrace was lined with potted trees and stand fans (the atmosphere was hot, dusty, and stuffy). There was a water tank on one side of the terrace and a pond on the other side. There were people labouring away to make the water tank appear antiquated; they were staining its walls with great diligence. In another shaded area of the terrace, the director and producers sat together with television monitors. There was a big light above that represented the moon. The lighting designer was using 'black chroma' (I was told) to create the illusion of a moonlit night where the shadows gently cascaded the terrace. I looked up to see the light grid (*tarafa*, as the crew called it) and saw a few men crouching and working high up near the ceiling. The camera was mounted on a moving scooter-like vehicle, on which the cameraperson moved around vertically and horizontally to figure out various camera angles for filming the scene.

There was one person sitting with a megaphone giving directions to the crew. The diversity of Mumbai was very visible on the set. There were women crouching on the ground polishing the marble tiles, attired in typical Maharashtrian style (*nauvari*) saris. Some of the men by their side had flowing beards and fez caps marking their Muslim identity. The director Sooraj Barjatya was a Jain, which I discovered during lunch as he followed a strict Jain vegetarian diet. Amidst these activities, a person came in to distribute a box full of *prasad* (sacred food that has first been offered to and consumed by a deity), which consisted of little pieces of delicious coconut. There were also aspirational actresses hanging out with their portfolios, as well as *chaiwalas* (tea servers) hovering around with cups of hot tea. A buzzing and unpredictable and chaotic Bollywood cinema world (that is never seen on screen) was unfolding in front of me.

I began visiting Film City regularly to see how the set was being put together for shooting one particular song sequence in *Vivah*. The scene was being choreographed by Jay Borade of *Hum Apke Hain Kaun?* fame. Although not a typical Bollywood dance sequence, it was a romantic scene that was based on postures, hand movements, and expressions based on Indian dance, Jay explained to me. The lines sung by Shreya Ghosal and Udit Narayan were 'Mujhe Haq Hai Tujhe Jee Bhar Ke Mein Dekhu' (I have the right to look at you to my heart's content); the music director was Ravindra Jain. Jay was choreographing the song on Sunita Shetty (his assistant, also a choreographer) and Vikram Borade (his assistant and son, and also a choreographer) (Figures 4.2 and 4.3). Sunita explained to me that the song is recorded first and then *masterji* (the name for male choreographers in Bollywood) conceptualizes the scene and puts the work on the assistant choreographer to figure out

Figure 4.2   Sunita Shetty and Jay Borade, Choreographers in Film City Studios, Mumbai
Source: Author.

FIGURE 4.3   Vikram Borade and Sunita at the Sets of *Vivah* in Film City
Studios, Mumbai
Source: Author.

the camera angles. This determines how the choreography will actually
appear on the screen. This is also useful for training the assistant who
gets to know how the master choreographer works. This is how (Sunita
explained) Bombay film choreographers were usually trained. While I
was sitting and talking with Jay and Sunita, the cameraperson was busy
setting the lighting on another dummy (man) who was lying on the
tiled floor covered with a white cloth. Sunita got up to replace the man
on the floor, while Vijay positioned himself above her. They held hands
in a lying position and Jay gave them directions to play with their hands
and use Vijay's fingers to trace and separate the bangles. The lines were:
'Chudiyan Gun-guna Ke Kya Kahe Sajana?' (What does the hum of the
bangles say my beloved?).

Jay was intensely focused on how the hands should be designed for
the camera. When he was ready, Amrita Rao, the Bollywood actress,
appeared. She freshened her makeup, added a coat of lipstick, and then

lowered herself down to a lying position where Sunita was before. Shahid Kapoor took Vikram's position. The shots were taken a few times. But they were not satisfactory. While Amrita and Shahid left to wait in their air-conditioned buses, Sunita took her original position on the floor. Jay explained the camera angle to her. He decided that the camera should be on the ground facing the hands at a right angle. But there was still dissatisfaction with the shot from the director Sooraj Barjatya who had been patiently watching the scene on a television monitor in a shaded area on the terrace. The angle apparently was incorrect and the movement of the bangles could not be seen on the screen. There was a break at this point. The changing of the camera angle meant the whole position—lighting, set, and so on—needed to be rearranged.

After all the readjustments, Sunita and Vijay lay down again on the floor. The cameraman panned the hands and the bangles as the song progressed. Jay explained again that Sunita's face should come into focus. He turned to me and explained that the posture they were striking on the floor and their hand movements were from Indian dance. 'See how the girl lies flat with her right leg folded and the boy lies next to her leaning and holding her left hand ... I have choreographed it like a dance sequence.' He further explained, 'the face and bangles need to be under focus, then the camera should catch the man looking at the woman. The woman's left hand then shifts and moves to his right shoulder. All these exchanges and locking of glances follow techniques of dance.' However, the shot was cancelled again. The angle was still not right. Jay decided that it was a compact shot and there was no need for two cameras. He explained that the problems are always with close-up shots: the distance from the face to the camera has to be measured carefully; the dance movement and camera movement need to be synchronized; the movements have to be meticulously choreographed. He said:

I find it much easier to choreograph group dancing with a lot of action. Moreover, for the close-ups you also need good actors, because the movements need to match the right facial expression. Then comes editing, this is where the polishing happens. The director gives the choreographer the authority to edit the shots. During editing you can see where you have made mistakes.

On this particular day the camera angles did not work for the terrace scene. The shots were taken innumerable times. The makeup artist touched up Sunita's makeup several times. The shots had to be perfect with her hair flying in some shots and not-so in some others. I visited Film City and the *Vivah* set a number of times to talk at length, have lunch with the crew, and see Sunita, Vikram, and Jay at work as the shooting progressed. I give a selective account of these conversations below to highlight how the choreographers saw the changing aesthetics and values associated with Bombay film dance.

Sunita Shetty (June 2006)

There is a lot of competition in the dance scene. People often pull others down if they see talent. I am lucky because I got the opportunity to be an assistant to the Bollywood icon Saroj Khan. I trained only in Indian folk styles and do not have a classical background. I often have to choreograph women in the film shows and music videos in very revealing clothes. It is because the director wants it that way. It is for an artistic reason; but these days the dancers flash their bodies because they look good. I come back home sometimes, think back, and feel that the scene I choreographed was simply vulgar. The only choreographic scope is with women wearing scanty clothes and doing western dance. In this kind of dancing, you cannot express feelings like in Indian dances; you only exhibit your body. I have only studied until the 10th standard. I had to drop out to support my family through dance. That is how I became an assistant to Saroj Khan, whom I really admire. I keep busy with my work and travel around the world. I will be going to Canada soon to work on a music video. But, I know that the demand will be for western style choreography.

Jay Borade (June 2006)

I learned western dances—Waltz, Tango, Rock and Roll, and Cha Cha—in Pune. I was from a military family and my father was a very good ballroom dancer. I worked as an assistant choreographer to Surya Kumar for many years. I have worked as an assistant for altogether 14 years. I was an assistant to Vijay Oskar in the film *Love in Goa* (1984). I have choreographed for about 300 films in Hindi (of course), Marathi, Bengali, Punjabi, Oriya, and Pakistani. But my main break came from *Hum Apke Hain Kaun?* Despite my success as a choreographer in Bombay cinema, I am not happy about what is happening with the so-called Bollywood dance. Nowadays people do not care about situation or context. There is no concept, no understanding of lyrics. I care about the lyrics and what movement should be associated with them. Now everyone is eager to make a fast buck. So, they just watch MTV and mix movements together. They only take a day to choreograph a music video. I always ask for the script so I can think about the situation and then I create the choreography. I can work on 10–12 films at a time because I have a system. I can keep track by creating a log [he drew the log on a piece of paper]. I write the serial number in the first column, then the lines of the lyrics, then the description of the situation, and then include the screenplay. It is not easy to conceive the situation. You have to consider the screenplay, lyrics, sets, and costumes to imagine the situation and then put the choreography together. Now, it is all about making money and taking shortcuts.

Although Jay Borade and Sunita Shetty were both quite critical of the changes in the Bollywood dance scene, one could argue that the particular de-contextualized aesthetics they describe have enabled the song and dance sequences to be a global success. The integration of movement/dancing, music, sets, camera angles, editing, and picturization (akin to MTV aesthetics) has created the aesthetics of 'remix'. These methodologies and techniques of 'remix' especially, as they pertain to movement vocabulary, are practised in classrooms and dance halls creating mediated embodiments, as I show below.

Dancing between Mumbai and Kolkata

'Jhik Jhik Ta, Jhik Jhik Ta, 1-2-3 and 1-2-3', resounded in my ears over and above the song bellowing from the stereo system in the room. The *tal* (metric) system was uniquely Bollywood, I thought to myself. I was in Vikram Borade's class in Shariq Hall in Andheri West. This was also where the famous Bollywood choreographer Ganesh Acharya held his classes (see Figures 4.4, 4.5, and 4.6). I was standing awkwardly in the

FIGURE 4.4   Ganesh Acharya Dance Academy, Mumbai, Where Dancers Rehearse Item Numbers
Source: Author.

FIGURE 4.5   Vikram Borade's Class, Mumbai
Source: Author.

FIGURE 4.6   Vikram Borade's Class, Mumbai
Source: Author.

corner of the studio with my notebook and micro cassette player trying to be unobtrusive and record what I was seeing, hearing, and experiencing. I was immersed in a world of new practices and new ways of knowledge transmission between dancing bodies.

The room I was in was a clean space with mirrored walls and an air conditioner. Vikram was teaching his dancers some Hip-Hop inspired movements. He was doing breaks and pops and throwing in some hand movements and gestures with the phrase he was showing. Vikram told his dancers, 'sab baatey bhul ke, bas ye baat yadh rakh' (Forget everything else, just remember these words). The girls looked like they were between 16 and 25 years of age. They all wore jeans, sweats, and sneakers. They were dressed in layers. The boys wore tight T-shirts that showed-off their buff bodies and toned muscles. Vikram was teaching them how to do partnering movements. Vikram was a very active choreographer. He had choreographed for major films, music videos, and dance shows. I could see that he was also an accomplished Bollywood dancer. He said he had assisted Raju Khan and choreographed the song 'Kinna Sona' by Nusrat Fateh Ali Khan. He said that he was choreographing an 'item number' for a film whose name had not been decided yet. He was not even aware of the story line except that a boy falls in love with a girl, but the boy was shy and the song was about his attitude to the girl. He said that the song was also about Bombay youth culture. In his words: 'I go with the lyrics and then I improvise. I visualize the song, then think about the steps, and then think about how the camera angle will work with the steps. It is about putting the best visual in the best way.'

Vikram constantly moved with the dancers to teach them a particular step or a gesture. The words of the song were ... 'chum le zara' (Kiss me a little). He instructed his dancers: 'put two fingers on your lips, one leg up, then extend the other free hand.' The hand gestures were simple and straightforward, he explained. He interpreted the word 'bhramar' (bee) with his index finger circulating.[10] The dancing was powerful, acrobatic, and unadorned with symbolism (there is no strict codification of Bollywood dance yet, although there are attempts at it by several choreographers). I followed Vikram from Shariq Hall in Andheri to Satyam Studios in Juhu to observe his teaching methods. As I was told during my fieldwork by Rajubhai, the secretary of Indian Film Dance Directors Association: 'There are no schools in Bollywood that will make you a choreographer, there are no degrees you can earn to establish your credentials, you have to learn on the job and serve as an assistant choreographer for years before you might get noticed. It's all luck and network.'

The movements intensified inside the studio. The movements had hip shakes, shoulder shakes, fast steps, bent knees, going on tiptoes, flaying hands, and still hands. The music was loud, very loud, and it slowly ate into my brains. I could not think or take notes. The DJ person sat in front of the stereo system and constantly manipulated the music. There was only loud music and frenzied moving bodies. The dancers rehearsed nonstop; taking short breaks and then they were back again repeating the movements (over and over again). The studio slowly filled with the fumes of deodorant and sweat. The dancers kept spraying themselves with deodrants to stay dry. They told me that they always carried it in their backpack. I stepped outside for a breath of fresh air. I started talking to a very young dancer who had stepped outside for a break. She told me she used to hate dance but she came into this 'line' after her mother (who used to be the sole earning member in her family) met with an accident. She said:

> I have no dance training. But I dance and rehearse twelve to thirteen hours every day. I love dancing item numbers. I also perform at

[10] The same word in classical dance is signified by specific mudras or hand gestures that take time (years, decades) to execute skilfully.

weddings. There is so much pressure ... sometimes you have to learn five dance items in two days. I earn Rs 2,000 to Rs 3,000 per day, about Rs 30,000 a month. It is better to be a dancer as there is always work. That is not the case for assistant choreographers like assistant-di [she pointed at Vikram's assistant Bhoomika]. Although the assistant is paid two and a half times more than the dancers, she has no regular work. We travel a lot. We just follow what the assistant-di tells us. We don't know what the dance is for, which film or music video. I am sixteen and can only dance until thirty. You need the figure and looks to make a dance career and by the time you reach thirty, you are out. I make the most of what I have. I have no college degree.

She gave me a sweet smile, finished her cigarette, I took a picture with her, and she ran back into the studio.

The 'remix' dances I was observing in Vijay Borade's classes were ubiquitous in 'maximum city' Mumbai's urban culture. Kolkata, where I went next, was far behind Mumbai in terms of commerce and industry and wealth, but was nonetheless also a hub for 'remix' dance practices and reality shows for the Bangla language audience. In Kolkata, the dance-spaces were tucked in various corners of the city, sometimes in the most unexpected places. I followed a few choreographers around as they held classes in a variety of contexts showing an incredible amount of dynamism, unpredictability, and flexibility but with a steady fixity of purpose. I had to reorganize my sense of time and place from the precise schedules of the American daily life I am used to. It was impossible to plan much as appointments and venues kept changing. This was a world of uncertainty and flexibility. This part of the story was the same both in Mumbai and Kolkata. The notion of fieldwork itself was challenged to suit this 'arrhythmic lifestyle' as Pandian (2013) eloquently expresses in his experience with filmmakers (2013). My frustration was echoed in my field notes.

Bhaskar came almost two hours late. I stood in front of the tall Exide building on Chowrangee Street in central Kolkata. This was a very busy part of the city, but traffic was light as it was a Sunday. As I waited, smells of *chops* and *pakoras* (flour fritters) wafted in the air. A pavement hawker was frying them on a kerosene stove. I was tempted to indulge and was debating the potential health hazards of such mouth-watering street snacks when Bhaskar arrived. He said he could not answer my phone calls as he was riding his bike; I noticed he was holding his helmet. I accompanied him inside the old building. This was a landmark commercial building that had seen better days. We climbed up five dark and dilapidated floors to reach a bright well-lit room. This was the front office of Shubela Production. Bhaskar explained that his classes here were part of this production house, which was trying to bring dance and films on the same platform. We sat in the front office that led to the studio and talked for a while. The room had posters of many dance forms and dancers including a poster that had Bhaskar in the center. The poster next to it showed Michael Jackson moonwalking, his hands thrown up, his face looking down and covered with a hat. There was also a poster with many different dance poses that read Jazz, Street, Lyrical, Modern, Hip-Hop, Ballet, and Contemporary (see Figure 4.7).

FIGURE 4.7 Bhaskar Raut's Classes Being Advertised inside Shubela Production, Kolkata
Source: Author.

The studio itself was big and impressive (compared to some others I have seen in Kolkata). One side of the room was mirrored and there was also a bathroom attached to the studio. The lack of toilet facilities in dance-spaces where dancers gathered and rehearsed for long hours was a problem that I became acutely aware of during my fieldwork. I personally experienced how the heavy use of toilets without proper sanitary mechanisms for long hours created unsavory sensory immersions for sweaty dancers and their choreographers, especially during the hot and humid summer days. Here too the deodorant or 'deo' came to the rescue.

The dancers in the room were from a variety of socioeconomic backgrounds. They arrived at different times and at one point it seemed to me that they kept trickling in. Bhaskar told me that the starting time of the class was 4:30. I looked at my watch. It was already 5:30. As I waited for people to arrive, I began chatting with one of Bhaskar's dancers in the office room. The young man told me he was from a small town. He accidentally met Bhaskar in Mumbai in a cancer hospital where his sister was getting treatment. He saw Bhaskar and immediately recognized him from a dance reality show. 'I saw dada who was on TV in front of me. He is on TV, which is a very big thing (eta khub boro bepar).' This young man was very eager to work with Bhaskar and take lessons from him. Bhaskar encouraged him to come to Kolkata and attend his classes and rehearsals despite the fact that he had no money to pay Bhaskar. He said he was so excited to see the dance studios here with big mirrors: 'We can actually see ourselves and correct the mistakes.' He said he was learning Contemporary dance earlier, but Bhaskar was teaching him the 'real' Contemporary. I came to know from him that Bhaskar also generously shared his tiny flat with dancers like him who came from out of town. Now the young man would be appearing on a Bangla TV channel Star Jalsha in October in a dance show called *Mega Jalsha*. The choreographer was Bhaskar, of course.

Bhaskar's repertoire was eclectic and open-ended like all the choreographers and dancers of reality TV. It included Contemporary, filmi or Bollywood, and Bharatanatyam. Other than Bharatanatyam, both Contemporary and Bollywood were fusion styles with no clear boundaries and often used Hip-Hop, Break, Salsa, Ballroom, and Contact. Bhaskar had created a name for himself as a choreographer in the reality show circuit in Bengal and its surrounding states. He held classes outside Kolkata, including Cooch Behar (in North Bengal) and in a community hall belonging to Haldia Petrochemicals in Haldia (an industrial small city in South Bengal). He told me he liked to recruit his dancers from small towns outside Kolkata as those students were more eager to learn and willing to face many hardships. 'They don't have the know-it-all [shobjanta] attitude of Kolkata-based dancers,' he said. Bhaskar said he was also putting an international tour together and launching a website.

The class eventually filled up. There were backpacks that eventually lined up at the back of the room and sat next to Bhaskar's bike helmet. The bike helmet, like the glove and sunglass, were the symbols of youth, mobility, and movement for a new generation of dancers and choreographers in urban centres such as Kolkata and Mumbai. The laptop in the corner played some techno music. Bhaskar had two assistants (a male and a female) who helped him teach. The dancers began moving with steps that looked like a mixture of Hip-Hop, floor work, head spins, and lunges. When I asked about the repertoire of movements he was using, Bhaskar told me he called it 'freestyle'. The class looked unstructured with hands-on and ad hoc teaching methods. Bhaskar repeatedly showed the head spin to a young boy by breaking it down part by part. I cringed a few times as they were on a mosaic floor that strained their necks. It looked painful. But what to do? Sprung wooden floors were a rarity in the city. The males in the group were eager to execute the move. The atmosphere in the class was casual and non-hierarchical. Bhaskar changed the music playing on the laptop in the corner from time to time but it appeared to me that the music was just being used as background filler and was unrelated to the movements.

During another visit to Bhaskar's class, I found him teaching without any music. The class was crowded with young males. Bhaskar gave precise instructions to the group, mostly in Hindi. He told me 'they are all coming from different places outside Kolkata such as Sodpur, Beharampur, Purulia,' and then he got busy with teaching. He showed them how to stretch one arm above their head with one arm to the side while reciting 1-2-3-4-5-6-7 and then how to drop to the floor on 8, then circle on the ground on their hips with legs split like scissors. He showed them how to quickly fall to the ground and hold the movement; 'hold', he shouted many times. His female assistant helped one male student hold his spine and stretch his legs. Bhaskar demonstrated how to rise from the floor and immediately go into motion: '1 and 2 and sashay and drop and hold with one leg up.' He repeatedly showed his students a phrase that included a drop to the floor, a turn on the floor using the hips as the pivot, then a head roll with legs split, rise up and take a little hopping step and turn and drop again and repeat This phrase was difficult for the dancers. He patiently demonstrated again and again and told his students to observe his spine and think of their hips as the point of a compass to turn, turn, and turn.

Another evening in Bhaskar's studio inside the Exide building, I observed him teaching a completely different movement vocabulary. He told me that the particular movement he was teaching was from Kalariyapattu (a difficult and old martial art tradition from Kerala). He called out 'kick up' and showed a forceful kick with legs reaching out and up to almost his temple. Then he added 'step back immediately with the right leg.' He then told his students to stretch their hands forward and touch the hands while they had one leg up. He added another movement to the leg that was already up ... a circular movement with the kick, then stepped back and then to the side and he shouted, 'hold'. The group observed him keenly. He suddenly pushed one of his students and said brusquely 'use force, show strength'. Bhaskar was on a roll. He added another movement that included a front kick, then a swinging back kick, then a half turn and then a full turn. He asked his students to show him the movements individually. They showed him their fall, reverse, get up, hold, and fall again. He talked incessantly. He said to his students that the person who taught him the Kalari movements came from Kerala. His name was Robi Josh, who was a small thin fellow, but had fantastic agility and was a powerful mover. He scolded them mildly: 'Please practice, do you practice at home?' One student asked how he could get lighter. 'Jog', he told him. I asked him whether these dancers were part of his performing group. He said that they were just his students. But some may be recruited. In his performing group, he added, they needed to know classical, folk, western, and Bollywood. Above all, they needed to be fit and flexible. He described to me how he slowly assembled his group while working in different cities and small towns.

The music blasted from another laptop in another dance studio in Kolkata. The youthful bodies moved to the music with shakes, breaks, jumps, twists, and turns. The instructor with a trendy cap on his head and a sleeveless tee shirt that revealed well-muscled arms shouted, 'drop to the floor'. The dancers clad in jeans and sneakers dropped horizontally on the floor from a vertical position with an easy slide. They moved constantly with furious energy and sweated profusely. The ceiling fan seemed decorative, wholly inadequate for the hot and humid air of a Kolkata summer. And then there was the ubiquitous laptop, a constant source of information. It was certainly one of the biggest investments for the choreographer whose class I was observing. Sajid explained the importance of the laptop for him:

> I look up movements by famous Bollywood dancers like Hrithik Roshan, and if a movement is appealing I copy and put it on my dancers. This is not a new invention. I personally learned a lot of moves from just

watching Michael Jackson videos. I copied a move then practiced a lot. I loved dancing and would practice for hours. I was always a dancer. Now I want to be a famous choreographer.

The dancers in his class came from a variety of backgrounds, not unlike the other classes I had visited. Many had Indian classical training, many had western training (though the term 'western' was nebulous and could mean anything from Hip-Hop and Salsa to Bollywood free style), and many were self-trained. Although the dancers I was observing physically resembled the backup dancers of Bollywood, they were mostly local dancers with dreams of making it to Bollywood. Their instructor (Sajid) was once a backup dancer in Bollywood but left because he wanted to be a choreographer. The dancers in the room were young, ambitious, flexible, and adept at learning any steps or movements presented to them (see Figures 4.8, 4.9, and 4.10). A very talented dancer and a participant on the television dance reality show *Dhum Machale* (which I explore in detail in Chapter 5) explained:

FIGURE 4.8   Sajid Jamal's Class, Kolkata
Source: Author.

FIGURE 4.9   The Billboard for Sajid Jamal's Class in Kabardanga, Kolkata
Source: Author.

FIGURE 4.10   A Rehearsal for a TV Reality Show, Kolkata
Source: Author.

I began with Ananda Shankar's school of modern dance. I then studied the classical dance style of Odissi for a long time. However, I was always attracted to western dance. I looked at ballet on television and studied it on my own. I also tried to do moves used by gymnasts. Television was a source of inspiration. Now I am studying to learn western dance.

Sajid, the instructor and choreographer who I was visiting, came into limelight from dance reality shows. He was mostly self-trained and his forte was Michael Jackson-style break dancing with Bollywood punches thrown in. The son of a seamstress, Sajid grew up in difficult socio-economic circumstances. His fame was symbolic of the democratic potential of dance reality shows. In his words:

> If you have talent it will come out in the reality shows. I like reality shows as it gave me a platform. People like me who lack backing needs such platforms. The laptop is most precious to me—it helps me to connect to Bollywood instantly and I can replicate some of the choreography. But I always try to be creative with movement.

I met Sajid again in Kabardanga (a neighbourhood of Behala in the far southern part of Kolkata) in a chaotic market area. Sajid had a class on the second floor of a building with a sign outside that said: 'Sajid's Dance Institute, perfect training center to be professional and Reality Show's western dance forms.' Then the board listed: 'Bollywood, Contemporary, Hip-Hop, Locking-Poping, Beeboying, Crumping, Pupet, Robotic, Tap, Salsa, Jazz, Chachacha, Latin.' The area was a very busy wet market area with a slaughterhouse situated right opposite Sajid's studio. The street lighting was thin and dim. Although far from Chowrangee and urban landmarks such as the Exide building, Sajid had attracted plenty of students here, many from far away. Sajid said he only taught his junior students here. He taught and performed with his senior students in central Kolkata, in Chandni. He told me he seldom goes to the classes held in south Kolkata where I first met him a few years ago. He proudly said that he had recently choreographed for the super hit reality show *Dance Bangla Dance* on Zee channel, his choreography got the first prize, and now his fortune was rising. He added that he had about 68 students.

Sajid's class in Kabardanga was a modest room with chairs lining one wall. The ceiling seemed to be made of asbestos (it was definitely not concrete) with wooden rods crisscrossing the tiles. The fans were hung low from the wooden rods. The room had big glass windows on two sides and they opened out to the busy streets. Sajid said that this particular class was meant for school-age students. The mothers of these children sat on chairs, waited patiently, and observed the class. Sajid played music from a portable CD player and danced with the remote in his hand. He counted 1-2-3-4 then 5-6-7-8 and showed how each count had a specific movement (I realized he had broken down the movements into their smallest segments to teach his students): they consisted of jumps, torso movements, head and neck movements. Some of the movements appeared to be simple and straightforward, almost like a drill exercise. But some were complicated, like lying on the floor face down, then springing back up and standing straight and dropping immediately with straight legs (certainly inspired by Hip Hop). There were times I saw them doing Hip Hop-inspired shoulder isolations. Some of the very young dancers in his class had aspirations of participating in the popular reality show *Dance Bangla Dance*. This particular reality show was a competition for children and young adults and had become the inspiration for the national reality show *Dance India Dance*.

Sajid's assistant worked individually with the kids. Some of them were able to remember and do the moves but some jumped around cluelessly. Sajid told me that he seldom diluted his movement vocabulary for kids. He wanted them to be exposed from an early age to difficult dance moves and expressions so that they were aware of his distinct style. I observed one little girl dancing with Bollywood-style facial expressions usually exhibited by 'item girls'. (This is usually considered very vulgar by most middle class Indians and many had expressed to me during academic conferences in India that their distaste for dance reality shows stems from such overt expression of sexuality by young children.)[11] Sajid said he usually taught using 'item numbers' so that his

---

[11] It should be noted here that the *abhinaya* or facial expressions associated with classical or rasa aesthetics in Indian dances is now replaced by the emphasis on choreography and group dances in general.

students learnt the 'item number' rather than a movement repertoire. He added that the movements he was teaching in the class were a mix of Bollywood, Hip-Hop, and Contemporary. He encouraged me to visit his class in Chandni in central Kolkata where he rehearsed with his professional group.

So I followed him to Chandni one day. Chandni was a bustling bazaar where, as the saying goes, you can buy anything from computer hardware to tiger's milk. I set out for Chandni around 7 in the evening, which is the peak rush hour in Kolkata, and it took me more than an hour to reach Chandni from the south of the city. Sajid was waiting for me in front of a restaurant. I spotted him immediately in the crowd; he had on his customary cap and sneakers and a bright purple shirt. I followed him to the back of the restaurant, climbed up dark stairs, leaving behind a bar on the mezzanine floor. I stepped inside a brightly lit, colorful studio with sparkling wooden floors and mirrored walls on one side. The walls were vivid orange and blue. There were shelves lining the room with children's toys and small statues of Hindu gods Ganesh and Saraswati. There was a music system in one corner. I wondered whether the space was also serving as a children's nursery school in the morning and the bar congregation in the evening. The hybrid/flexible functionality of the dance spaces I visited reflected the hybrid aesthetics of the dances being taught there.

Sajid's group was already rehearsing when we entered. There was an almost equal number of males and females in the group. The regional diversity of the group became evident as they started introducing themselves to me. The males were mostly college dropouts and from working class backgrounds. Some told me they had to drop out of school due to financial difficulties. There was one young man who had never been to any school or college and earned a living from sweeping streets. The men said they used the money they got from dancing to help their families. They said they could make up to Rs 3,000 per month from dancing (a big difference from the earnings of the Mumbai dancers); sometimes it could be more. The males in the group seemed to be harder up financially than the females and they seemed to have no prospects of going to college, whereas some of the females were in college but had no interest in academics. Sajid added that all the dancers in his group were extremely hard working (*bahut mehnat karta*) but were from difficult financial situations (*paisa nahi hai*). They all seemed to have high regard for their leader, Sajid.

During my repeated visits to Chandni, I discovered the range of dancers who came to Sajid for him to choreograph their dance pieces. Some came to prepare for dance competitions, some for dance shows, and some came even for school curricula. Once I saw a young gymnast who had come to Sajid for him to design a choreography for her gymnastics competition. Sajid created his own mashup of several 'item numbers' on which he choreographed the dance pieces. His students learned the movements during the mashup process and everything was spontaneous and improvised. For instance, on one occasion, dancing to the hit 'item number' 'Sheila Ki Jawani' (Sheila's youth) from the Bollywood film *Tees Maar Khan*, the dancers used a wide range of styles from hip shakes, breaking, and popping, to splits, floor work, glide and heel-toe (Sajid used these terms for the movement vocabulary). In another song composed by Rahul Dev Burman *Duniya Mein, Logon Ko....Monica Oh My Darling* from the old Bombay film *Apna Desh* (My Country), with a pacey tempo and rock and roll beats, the dance vocabulary was a mix of Bollywood moves with shake and shimmy. Some of the movements looked like the original dancing in the scene in the movie, but some were Sajid's innovations. The dancers stood on the side and observed the movements before trying them. They all seemed to have a good rapport with each other and helped each other to learn the moves correctly. They all had great respect for Sajid, not only as their teacher, but also as a friend and someone who took care of their needs, financially and emotionally.

Outside Sajid's class in Chandni, a few mothers waited in the small and dark landing of the building. One mother, who I had also met in Kabardanga, brought her little girl to Chandni so she could improve by observing the older dancers. She told me she lived in Belur, an older industrial suburb north of Kolkata, a jute mill town where almost all the mills had closed. She had to take the train and auto for about three hours to come to class in Kabardanga, in the far south of the city. She wanted her daughter to excel in dance. She said that success can come from any source these days and her daughter was learning many kinds of dances, such as classical, Tagore, and Bollywood. The mothers echoed the dancers' sentiments that reality shows can open up chances for their children. That is, they could be 'someone' by participating in the shows; they may become a choreographer someday, and could even become famous. 'If you are on TV you are seen, if you are seen you are famous.' They all said the same thing. No doubt the fame they referred to here was associated with the 'celebrity culture' of Bollywood and the TV industry. Next, I visited the sets of auditions for *Dance India Dance* to further chart the journey of such dreams of stardom and celebrity.

Dance India Dance Auditions

I had to break into the scene of the *Dance India Dance* audition in Kolkata rather abruptly as I came to know about it just the day before. Not having any prior connections with any of the organizers, I had to use some cajoling and coaxing, but I was determined to utilize this unexpected opportunity. I was learning to embrace the uncertainties of my field-work experiences. Things happened unexpectedly and schedules had to be rescheduled. The auditions were taking place in the Swabhumi Heritage Plaza next to the eastern bypass. A gate had been constructed with the banner of *Dance India Dance* with large pictures of the three judges of the show. There were throngs of people camping outside from 3 am (I was told that thousands had arrived from the northeastern states of India). Fast food snack vendors had provided food and sustenance throughout the night. It had been a long night I could tell, as I saw the contestants and their friends, teachers, and families sprawled all over the parking lot. Some were reclining on their luggage and many were sleeping in various awkward positions. Despite the enormous numbers, it was an orderly crowd (see Figure 4.11).

The celebrity judges for *Dance India Dance* had arrived from Mumbai: Terence Lewis, Remo D'Souza, and Geeta Kapoor. They were now household names. Terence Lewis specialized in contemporary dance and had trained in Alvin Ailey American Dance Theater and the Martha Graham Center for Contemporary Dance in New York, U.S. He had choreographed for Bollywood films such as *Lagaan* (2001) and *Jhankaar Beats* (2003). Remo D'Souza was not only a successful dance choreographer but had also directed the film *Anybody Can Dance* (popularly known as ABCD, which later led to a sequel ABCD 2) which featured two *Dance India Dance* contestants. Remo D'Souza was self-trained and considered Michael Jackson his guru (he learned his moves from watching

FIGURE 4.11   Audition Setting for *Dance India Dance*, Kolkata
Source: Author.

his videos). He was first noticed during an *All India Dance Competition* (http://www.india-forums.com/celebrity/9936/remo-dsouza/biography/India-Forums.com). Geeta Kapoor's elevation to stardom followed a different and more traditional route for Bollywood choreographers. She became famous by assisting the famous choreographer Farah Khan, who was an assistant to the Bollywood icon Saroj Khan (Geeta had shared her career trajectory with me during my interactions with her in Mumbai).

The inner courtyard of Swabhumi was swarming with contestants dressed in a variety of dance costumes. Some were in full classical dance regalia like Bharatanatyam and Manipuri, some wore bodysuits with eyes painted black like raccoons, and some wore an eclectic mix of long skirts (*ghagra*) with short blouses and tights. The costumes and makeup reflected the mix of styles and genres, which were as randomly and innovatively put together as some of the movement repertoires I was about to observe. There were contestants hanging out dejectedly outside the audition area and some eagerly spoke to me. A group of boys from Sikkim were disappointed by the entire organization of the audition and the lack of fairness in the process of selection. They said they were all self-trained Hip-Hop artists and they had come from far and waited long hours only to be given less than half a minute of time for their audition. They claimed that the selection process was rigged. They were cut off in the preliminary rounds by one of the past winners, now turned junior judge for *Dance India Dance*. They claimed that the judges already had their favourites. A Bharatanatyam dancer said that she had been trying her luck in several reality shows and thought that the process was fair. She announced that she was not going to give up her dream and would win some day and be on TV.

I was smuggled inside by one of the crewmembers into the privately sealed off space for the *Dance India Dance* auditions. This was a big spacious area where multiple TV sets hung and various cameras panned and focused on the contestants on the stage. The raised stage area had (*Dance India Dance*) written prominently across the backdrop. The judges sat at a distance from the stage to observe and give comments. In the next layer sat the audience in a raised makeshift gallery. I sat with the technicians on the ground behind the audience and we formed the last layer of observers. The contestants were all performing solo pieces. The judges gave them comments after their round was over; they were words of appreciation and/or criticism: 'you have to work on your balance, there are some problems with your release in the back, I liked your flexibility', and sometimes they said the most coveted words 'you are selected'. These words were always accompanied by loud squeals from the participants as they ran up to the judges for a quick *pranam* (gesture for showing respect). The audience exuberantly applauded. They were often asked to clap louder and show more emotion. This selection process continued until late evening and the judges were exhausted. One by one, 64 contestants were selected and the judges announced that the mega audition would be held in Mumbai on 3 December.

This event was like many other auditions of reality shows that are regularly organized in various cities of India and abroad. *Dance India Dance* was a major reality show on Zee TV. To be seen on TV as a contestant would be a huge accomplishment for the young aspiring dancers. Many of whom I spoke to believed that to win a *Dance India Dance* contest would be a sure ticket to stardom. A ticket that they believed would be theirs someday. The constant movement, running around, unpredictability and the ability to improvise both in the dance contexts and in real-life situations created the 'copy and paste' dance embodiment of 'remix' aesthetics. The new generation of dancers and choreographers of reality shows such as *Dance India Dance* represented the new embodiments of an aspirational emotion.

But there are important questions to consider. How far does the framework of 'embodiment' go in analysing the shifts in dance training and the shaping of affect/desire in contemporary India? How are subjectivities shaped through this mobile and hybrid bodily training that is yet to have a stable identity or a name? And how do all these ideas mesh with the concept of 'remix'?

'Remix' works in several layers: first, in the process of image-making through set building, movement, editing, and camera angles and so on in places like Film City Studios in Mumbai. Then, in the dance halls of Mumbai and dance classes and studios in Kolkata, where students learn 'item numbers' from choreographers such as Vikram Borade and Bhaskar and Sajid, who teach hundreds of students in various locations; here the embodiment of 'remix' is accomplished through bodily training in a variety of danced styles but mostly through packaged 'item numbers'. Next, on the sets of *Dance India Dance* where participants perform 'item numbers' to be selected as contestants and begin their journey to 'celebrity-hood' someday. 'Remix' here symbolizes the aesthetics of consumption and aspirations of celebrity-hood. In other words, I argue that 'remix' is the new emotion of aspiration that creates a cosmopolitan hybrid Indian identity.

'Remix' is also reflected in the dance movements that are mixed—a variety of dance vocabularies during classes and rehearsals for shows or workshops are lifted by choreographers from YouTube and other media and using a 'copy and paste' technique and choreographed/pasted on the bodies of the dancers. But, at the same time, the choreographers also innovate and improvise. They introduce new movements so that the dancing bodies remain porous and flexible to learn new techniques and embody images that may appear from any visual world. The codified bodily techniques of classical Indian dance or bhava-rasa has no relevance for this new generation of dancers as their identities perpetually negotiate the 'remix' images they encounter in their classes and media. Their dance practice of 'remix' means porosity, flexibility, hybridity, and fluidity and cannot be attached to any iconography of dance. 'Copy and paste' embodiment through dance belongs to no particular cultural domain or identity as the dancers inhabit multiple locations and embrace hybrid dance styles. Appadurai's (1997: 44) argument resonates here: 'Culture is now less what Pierre Bourdieu would have called habitus (a tacit realm of reproducible practice and dispositions) and more an arena for conscious choice, justification, and representation.' One could further argue that culture and cultural identity are now more about flexibility, contingency, and manipulation, as I show in the next chapter, than some adherence to unconscious habits or preexisting or prescribed category of social identity. Dance reality shows, and reality shows in general, produce a kind of human plasticity that is more real than the real, where dancers constantly negotiate the virtual and actual in a world where the screen dominates every aspect of experience.

5

Mediated Subjectivities

The symbiotic relationship between Bombay films/Bollywood and television has a long history. Television has carried film programming from its early days and promoted the song and dance sequences from Bombay films through popular shows like *Chitrahaar* on Doordarshan. I remember that as a child one of my favorite shows that I saw on the only channel on TV was *Chitrahaar* and the occasional Hindi movie my parents deemed were suitable for my susceptible mind. That was then. Now there are hundreds of channels in several languages, of which the vast majority carry entertainment programming—movies, serials, their derivative material like film, music and celebrity news, and reality shows.

This chapter begins with a brief look at the struggle to unshackle Indian television from state control before focusing more squarely on the emergence of television dance reality shows such as *Just Dance* and *Dhum Machale* on national and local television networks. So, the first section titled 'Television History and Autonomy' concentrates on the recent development and explosion of cable networks on television after a long period of state control and the second section, 'Remix and Dance Reality Shows', analyses the spread of reality shows through various media networks. It connects the industry of Bollywood to television and other electronic media and focuses on two reality shows, one regional and one national, to describe and analyse their contents. The third section, 'Digitized Desires', segues into life histories of a few reality show dancers and choreographers to get some insight into their personal struggles, aspirations, and achievements. The purpose is to focus on the televisual and lived experiences of the dancers and choreographers that connect the production of spectacles on screen to their everyday lives. I am concerned with how individual subjectivities are forged by new desires and everyday life experiences and how the embodiment of aspirational desires is shaped by technological mediations and the culture of celebrity.

Television History and Autonomy

The question of autonomy versus state control was central in the policy debates over Indian television for a long time. The earlier hegemony of the state broadcaster Doordarshan was challenged after the economy began to be liberalized from the mid-1980s. The development of Doordarshan for 'education, information, and entertainment' was the guiding principle of television from its inception in 1959 (Mankekar 1999; Gupta 1998; Ninan 2000; Kumar 2006). The creation of Doordarshan (like Bombay films) was integral to the larger nationalist project of building a modern nation state. The 'holy triad' of public service broadcasting—education, information, and entertainment—was reiterated by the various committees formed by the government to design guidelines for Doordarshan programming (Gupta 1998: 35). Although Doordarshan as a prominent arm of the state had the lofty goals of maintaining 'territorial integrity, national integration, secularism, maintenance of public order, and upholding the dignity and prestige of Parliament, state legislatures, and the judiciary', it was not until 1982 that it attained real significance as the government's pre-eminent media institution (Ninan 2000: 8). Accordingly, in 1982, Doordarshan introduced the nationwide coverage called the 'National Programme' with the explicit goal of disseminating news, information, and entertainment for shaping a modern national culture (Mankekar 1999).

The overall aim of television was to disseminate elite culture through education and raise cultural taste and values. Classical Indian dance and music as markers of Indian civilizational heritage were regularly featured in the national programming for upholding a pan-Indian national identity (Chakravorty 2008). However, the gradual decentering of state control of TV and the proliferation of cable networks and satellite broadcasting disrupted the hegemony of Doordarshan. These networks fragmented the viewership and diversified the cultural forms and products disseminated through television. The growth of commercial channels (that soon became networks with multiple channels and later outlets on the internet and other new media) such as Star, Zee, Sony, Sun TV, Eenadu TV (ETV) since 1991 has been staggering. The liberalization of Indian economy, which took off in the 1990s, coincided with the advent of satellite television in India. This cultural shift started when a then-obscure network called Satellite TV Asian Region or STAR TV began broadcasting over Asia from Hong Kong. Shanti Kumar (2006: 7) writes:

> By the 1990's, almost every transnational satellite television network worth a name—CNN, the Cartoon Network, ESPN, Disney, and Discovery channel set up shop in Asia.... In 1996, a Goldman Sachs report revealed that in the vast Asian markets, STAR TV had quickly emerged as the largest transnational television network, with an estimated potential of fifty-three million households.

But channels such as Zee TV quickly countered the English language domination of Star TV and competed with it for capturing the attention of the large Hindi-speaking population in India and the diaspora. There soon emerged other players to tap into the vast linguistically and culturally diverse Indian market. Commercial channels such as Sun TV and ETV started doing programming in regional languages to cater to the vernacular interests of the viewers (Kumar 2006). With the spread of commercial networks and deepening of the liberal economy came cultural shifts led by an emerging generation of postcolonial cultural producers and consumers. Kumar writes that 'a younger, more urban, Anglophile, and technophile generation took charge of producing a new, more cosmopolitan image for Indian television' (Kumar 2006: 34).

The cultural autonomy of television became an important agenda for the new television elite and the Prasar Bharati Bill became an important milestone. The struggle was on to free the airwaves from both the state control and the commercial forces controlled by a few private corporations. The Ministry of Information and Broadcasting set up the Sengupta Committee to suggest revisions to the Prasar Bharati Act which was passed by Parliament in 1990 but shelved by the Congress party when it came to power (Kumar 2006: 45).

Questions on government regulation regarding programming and distribution of satellite and cable television channels in India remained central to the debate on autonomy. As increasing numbers of national, transnational, and translocal satellite and cable channels began competing with state-sponsored networks, the debate regarding autonomy intensified. The introduction of transnational satellites created a marked change in national television programming. The number of channels that became newly available offered viewers, for the first time, the ability to choose between various television programs. In just five years, India went from having a single state-sponsored television channel to 69 nationally available channels (Cullity 2002: 410, quoted in Pathak 2014: 322). This, in turn, created a huge shift in cultural production that relied more on advertising and marketing budgets than on creating a national identity and consensus. The production of slick images and visual texts became the hallmark of television productions.

For example, NDTV, one of the most popular and well-regarded channels that had a market share of around 30 per cent, the highest among English television news channels, forayed into the infotainment sector with NDTV Imagine (now defunct) and NDTV Good Times. The latter is a lifestyle channel largely targeting young well-heeled Indian audiences with travel shows, food and fashion shows, lifestyle shows, and 'news' about Bollywood.

Needless to say, the arrival of cable networks not only created significant shifts in the narratives of modernity and identity in India, but, more specifically, had a very negative impact on the beaming of classical Indian dance programming on state-controlled Doordarshan. As commercial dance programs such as *Foot Loose* and *Boogie Woogie* hit cable networks in the 1990s, audiences started turning away from the didactic programming on Doordarshan to this new kind of commercial dance genre where Bollywood, Classical, Folk, Rap, Break, and Disco were packaged for consumption by the young. These shows followed a dance competition format with jazzy sets and disco lighting and a panel of celebrity judges. For instance, in *Boogie Woogie*, which is the longest-running dance talent show in India (but with big gaps in the late 1990s and early 2000s), Bollywood dancer/choreographer/actor Javed Jaffrey worked as the permanent celebrity judge. Here, performers as young as six or seven amused the audience with spicy numbers incorporating everything from Hip-Hop to Kathak. There were no cash prizes for the performers but heaps of applause from the judges and a live audience. The popularity of *Boogie Woogie* forged an alternative narrative of dance in India that was for everyone, both experts and amateurs, and that began to release Indian dance from the austere conventions of classicism. These transformations ushered in significant changes in values and tastes of dance aesthetics that could no longer be bounded by the past codes and conventions of classicism (Chakravorty 2008).

Remix and Dance Reality Shows

As I showed in the earlier chapters, dance reality shows on television form a growing genre of dance practice in India, which fuses Bollywood freestyle with western forms and traditional Indian dances such as classical and folk. A new aesthetics of continuous 'remix' (which cross-cuts classical and folk, Bollywood, and other hybrid forms that exist in-between) is replacing the past codes and affective experiences of Indian dances associated with bhakti (devotion), bhava (feeling, mood), and rasa (aesthetic emotion). These shifts, in turn, are changing the notions of 'Indianness' and Indian national identity (Indian national identity and classical dances are closely linked and have been discussed by many dance scholars since the 1980s).

'Remix' is an element of technological change as much as it is enabled by it. The 'remix' genre is associated with dance forms like Break and Hip-Hop that embrace notions of play, innovation, and mixing as they travel globally and morph into different forms (Osumare 2002). This practice is now integral to Bollywood and dance reality shows. It expresses a postmodern aesthetic of decontexualization, hybridity, and porosity. The cultural significance of the 'remix' genre embodied by the deejay (DJ) is represented in the hit film *Rang De Basanti* (2006) (Sundar 2014). Sundar writes that the deejay has historically operated at the interstices of at least four media industries in India: music, radio, film, and television. The DJ is the music designer who can be considered the driver of the remix genre. By focusing on *Rang De Basanti*, she argues that Indian history is incomplete without films, sound, song, and music. She re-conceptualizes the notion of history through the framework of aurality liberated from the linearity of historical text. In her words (Sundar 2014): 'casting itihasa as a remix unmoors the concept from its Indian and Hindu foundations. Itihasa is not just the realm of gods and ancient princes anymore, but that of Bhangra, Rai, and Bollywood.'

The 'remix' genre is now designing new dancing bodies that are no longer bound by geographical boundaries or boundaries between high and low culture. In this form and practice of dance, high and low, classical and folk, and Indian and other cultural forms combine and recombine to produce hybridity. I have suggested in the previous chapters that 'remix' is a quintessential postmodern embodiment of hybridity/ pastiche in which the lines between culture and commodity are blurred (Jameson 1991, 1998; Harvey 1989). I suggested that the experience of 'remix' could be explained as the indeterminacy of the body in postmodernism as posited by Thomas Csordas (1994: 6).

Analysing the body as the ground or site of culture as proposed by Csordas sheds acute light on some of the fundamental shifts in Indian society today. The dancing in reality shows is a heightened expression of this ongoing transformation and precarity. The most important aspect of this turbulent uncertainty is the spread of media and electronic communication due to the liberalization of the Indian economy (Appadurai 1997; Mankekar 2015). The embodiment of Indian dance is now deeply engaged in this burgeoning visual culture of new media, Bollywood, and new consumers. It has also given Indian dance, along with Bollywood, increased global significance. According to Daya Kishan Thussu (2008: 97):

> The combination of national and transnational factors, including deregulation of the media and communication sectors, the availability of new delivery and distribution mechanisms, as well as growing corporatization of the film industry, have contributed to [the] global visibility of popular Indian cinema.

The global prominence of Bollywood and its spread as a culture industry has influenced all aspects of culture, including dance. Its popularity arguably began with the film *Hum Apke Hain Kaun?* a musical that focused on two weddings, and that played for almost a year, grossing more than $30 million, a fabulous figure at the time (discussed in

Chapter 3). The expansion of the Bollywood market to the US, Canada, the UK, the Middle East, and East Asia followed, and Bollywood became a hallmark of successful global marketing.[1]

The dominance of Bollywood cinema over all aspects of cultural production deemed Indian—especially music, dance, and fashion—is particularly significant and linked to a 'cultural conglomeration involving a range of distribution and consumption activities from websites to music cassettes, from cable to radio', writes Ashish Rajadhyaksha (2008: 20). The dramatic expansion of television since the early 2000s, along with the emergence of cable networks such as Zee, Sony, and Star, have provided publicity engines for the rhizomatic circulation of Bollywood films, and especially the song and dance sequences. In fact, the song and dance sequence (renamed 'item number' in the 1990s) is a central aspect of Bollywood's culture industry today, featuring the ubiquitous dancing girl known as the 'item girl'.

The song and dance sequences in Bollywood films or 'item numbers' are like music videos that are detached from the films (as I have shown in Chapter 3) and circulate as autonomous products. They are released months before the film is released via many electronic outlets including YouTube and iTunes. They also appear on the dozens of television programs that exist simply to advertise Bollywood and its celebrity culture; and circulate on video, cable, and DVD. They also are 'remediated' through dance reality shows to amplify the processes of reinvention and circulation. 'Remediation is the repurposing of media from one context to another; it is a transfer of content from one format to another,

---

[1] During my fieldwork in Mumbai, John Mathew, a Bollywood director who is known for his film *Sarfarosh* had explained to me the importance of networking and marketing for Bollywood films. He had said that producers now spent a lot more money on marketing films than on making films, which is very different from past practices.

thereby making media new, and making new media' (Novack 2010: 41). Novack also connects this process of remediation to the making of modern cosmopolitan subjects. Dance reality shows use the 'item numbers' in a new format, they are re-choreographed and packaged to make them a televisual product to be consumed across various boundaries—local, national, and international. This process of simultaneous repackaging and innovation was evident in the dance studios and classes I visited and described in the previous chapter. Together they bestow a unique dimension to consumer culture in India that is specific to dance as an artistic form. At the same time the format and packaging of dance reality shows make them a televisual product that is a mobile cultural form, is modular, and has a global reach. The astonishing proliferation of reality shows in general in India and all over the world has been summarized as 'The Real As Global' by Sen (2014: 204). Remixing and remediation, I propose, are ultimately both aspects of the global in producing hybrid and modern cosmopolitan subjects.[2]

The popularity of both 'item numbers' and dance reality shows aid the spread of Bollywood as a culture industry, the processes of remediation, and the Bollywoodization of Indian culture (Rajadhyaksha 2008; Novack 2010). As a result, the Bollywood-inspired remixed dances of the reality shows have emerged as arguably the most visible cultural products of India's liberalized economy. In fact, the dance reality shows can be considered platforms which present the Bollywood 'item numbers'. It is a part of a process that brings Bollywood industry even closer to the audience, not just as passive consumers but also as active partakers in the making of a transnational celebrity culture.[2]

---

[2] The Bollywood choreographer Remo D'Souza recently said that dance reality shows have changed the Bollywood dancing style in recent years. Therefore, the symbiotic nature of the two industries continues in new directions. 'After we started that reality show which I was a part of long back, the whole scenario of dancing has changed in India. Everyone was educated

Naach Dhum Machale

ETV is a Bangla language regional television channel based in Kolkata. The show *Naach Dhum Machale* was launched on this channel in 2008 and continued through 2009; being aired during prime time three times a week. It was designed to be a concoction of humour, dance, emotional drama, and artistic talent. The staging of the show was set up like a Bollywood song and dance event with strobe and technicolored lighting and a backdrop that used elaborate lighting designs to create the gaudy visual extravaganza of Bollywood stage shows. The costumes were wide-ranging and full body painting was often used for dramatic effect. The music was generally film-inspired and the songs were in either Bangla or Hindi. The presentations were short and concise and followed the format of the 'item numbers' in Bollywood. A panel of celebrity judges sat on one side of the stage. Two of them were well-known choreographers in the city, Tanushree Shankar and Alokananda Roy, and the third was a film director. Each contestant, who was selected after many rounds of auditions, was assigned a choreographer and provided with backup dancers for choreographing the pieces. Before each dance sequence, the host introduced the dancer and her choreographer. They walked in side by side, often holding hands to the applause of a live audience. Then the camera cut to the dance sequence with the spotlight on the dancer. The dance sequences had interludes during which one or two co-hosts provided comic relief, often creating a comic super-text that ran counter to the dance narrative on stage.

---

about dancing and they came to know about all the dance forms in India. Because of that, the film industry has also changed, its dancing has changed.' Available at http://indianexpress.com/article/entertainment/television/dance-shows-on-tv-changed-bollywoods-dancing-style-remo-dsouza/.

The emphasis of the show from the very beginning was not on displaying proficiency in one technique, but on versatility. The styles ranged from African, Jazz, Tagore, Folk, Hip-Hop, Bharatanatyam, Kathak, and Bollywood. The show had certain themes such as 'street scenes', 'courtesan', 'cabaret', and so on, and they displayed a particular choreography on a particular dancer. The song selections were made by the choreographers to focus on the themes. The show provided a televised platform for unknown dancers and choreographers, the majority of whom would otherwise have never had such an opportunity.

Naach Dhum Machale arguably created a polysemy of intertextual experiences that facilitated competing perceptual registers. The sense of time and space was multidimensional, since the show was not live, but pretended to be. It was even more confusing for me because I began watching the show in India and continued in the U.S. via satellite television. The television screen was just one of the frames through which I watched. The other frame was the actual stage in the TV studio. On that stage, the emotional experience for the viewer ranged from being obviously contrived to utterly spontaneous. And the most commonly contrived emotion was the collective experience of loss felt by viewers, judges, and participants alike during the elimination rounds.

The importance of the collective experience was emphasized in the show. The hosts always talked about the elimination rounds in terms of losing a family member. The dancers showed their ties to 'tradition' and to the elders in society by doing pranam or bowing to the stage and to the judges (as their gurus). They embraced their choreographers as if they were best friends and longingly asked the audience to vote for them. Despite the competitive nature of the show, the importance of family and friends was continuously highlighted, as the camera frequently focused on family members in the audience who also did short interviews during the show.

At the same time, the pressures of competing and winning were obvious for the dancers and choreographers. After the judges announced the points, the contestants addressed the audience directly: 'I am Sanjukta Ray, my code is 12, if you have liked my performance please dial this number and send me your support.' There were interviews with them after they lost in a round where they spoke candidly to the television audience about the problems they faced during practice sessions and performances. Sometimes the dancers spoke about their difficulties with a particular choreographer or the choreographers complained about some participants. The dialogical style added to the immediacy and 'liveness' of the episodes. Altogether, the episodes were emotionally charged and despite differences showed a collective bonding.

The participants all played to win. The final round carried a heightened sense of emotional drama that created a palpable resonance across and through television screens (giving new meaning to Raymond Williams' 'televisual flows'). It created a 'community of affect' as suggested by Kavka (discussed in Chapter 2) through the viewer's identification with the performers who in turn identified with the celebrity judges or aspired to be like them. Although Kavka, Mazarella and others separate affect from emotion and argue that affect is just about surface sensation whereas emotion has meaning, I posit here that affect/emotion converged in these televisual experiences through the material awards of cash, cars, or other luxury goods. For instance, in *Dance Dhum Machale* there was a 'viewer's choice' award that was different from the actual prize for the show. It was worth Rs 7 lakh (enough money to buy a small apartment in an outer suburb of Kolkata). But, as one of the contestants reminded the judges and the audience after she lost in the final round, it was never about the money, but about succeeding/winning. The desire to succeed here was expressed through the aspirational emotion of 'remix' dances and participating in reality shows. The contestants came mostly from middle and lower middle-class backgrounds and spoke constantly about their aspirations of becoming famous. This dance reality show was their pathway to belong to the glamorous world of celebrity culture.

The dancers (although local) were excellent and versatile, and Sanjukta Ray, who won the competition, ultimately went on to be the winner of *Nach Baliye* (2009), a dance reality show on the national television channel Star Plus with Bollywood choreographers like Farah Khan as celebrity judges (Figure 5.1). Farah Khan expressed her delight after seeing Sanjukta's performance to the song 'Zara Zara Kiss Me' (*Race*) with these words: 'What are you doing here, Sanjukta? You should be on an international reality platform.'

Naach Dhum Machale was a low budget reality show with local dancers and local celebrity judges on a regional channel. Despite such local moorings, the representation of the dancing bodies in the show was far from local. They displayed a variety of dance styles from all over the globe including Indian classical and folk. These dancing bodies were no longer bound to a singular notion of Indian identity or tradition associated with sringara rasa or bhakti (of the Indian classical concert dances). The display of a multitude of styles performed by the

FIGURE 5.1   Sanjukta Ray in *Naach Dhum Machale*
Source: Author.

agile bodies created a panorama of desire and affect. The psychedelic lighting swirling around the dancing bodies wove a fantasyland of light, colour, movement and spectacle that beckoned the audience and the competitors alike to the dazzling and illusive world of celebrity culture. The televisual images of the dancing produced a packaged commercial aesthetic (or 'commodity aesthetic') that tended to blur the distinction between experiencing emotion and consuming spectacular images.

The aesthetics of 'remix' is ultimately an expression of erotic desire related to the consumption of spectacle. Purnima Mankekar (2004) has examined the role of the erotic in contemporary Indian culture, especially the relationship between the erotic and the consumption of commodities and the reconfiguration of gender, family, caste, and nation. She details the eroticization of commodities through images, texts, billboards, television, and films in the late twentieth century that stimulate the onlooker to desire, possess, or purchase the product. She argues for a convergence between erotic desire and the desire to con-sume and calls it a 'commodity affect' (echoing the idea of 'commod-ity aesthetics'). There is a symbiotic relationship between advertising, television, films, and the production of the 'commodity affect'. The pleasure of consumption is not just about acquiring something, but about gazing upon that thing and desiring to display it. Thus, a new kind of subjectivity is produced: an active, sexual, consuming subject full of desires (Mankekar 2004). This new aspirational, consumerist subject is produced in abundance through dance reality shows such as *Naach Dhum Machale* on ETV Bangla, despite its low production values compared to national shows such as *Just Dance*.

Just Dance

Just Dance aired on Star Plus during the summer of 2011. It ran every Saturday and Sunday from 9 pm, a prime viewing time. It arrived with a lot of hype as it featured Hrithik Roshan, a Bollywood megastar, also known for his dancing talent. He was one of the celebrity judges for the show along with two hit Bollywood choreographers Vaibhavi Merchant and Farah Khan. They provided the brand identity for *Just Dance*. Hrithik Roshan was making his television debut with the show and he was reputed to have been paid the highest ever for any television appearance until that year, a whopping Rs 17.5 million per episode. The show won the award for the best reality show from the Indian Television Academy. International corporations like Maruti Suzuki and Cadbury sponsored the show. The winner of *Just Dance* received a Maruti Suzuki Swift car plus a cash prize of Rs 10 million. The show held auditions in several big cities in the U.S. and the U.K. such as London and New York, plus, of course, Delhi, Mumbai, and Kolkata, as well as in many small towns in India. Fifty-two dancers were recruited after auditioning some 40,000. Ultimately, 13 dancers were invited to Mumbai to participate in the run up to the grand finale. The stakes were high. The competition was fierce.

There were several preview shows aired on Star Plus to create the build-up to the final weeks of the show. There were personal interviews with the contestants highlighting where they came from, their humble backgrounds, their family members, their passion for dance and their struggles and aspirations to pursue their dream of being on *Just Dance*. The most important factors were their desire to meet Hrithik Roshan, to win, and to become a famous dancer and a choreographer. The signature Hinglish song ran over and over again as the show progressed: *sab kuch bhul ke, just dance* (forget everything else and just dance). The judges Vaibhavi Merchant and Farah Khan gave out certificates of *Just Dance* to contestants who qualified to proceed to the next level of the competition.

In one such episode, we (the television audience) met a contestant called Chhibramau who had arrived from a semi-rural town in Kannauj in the state of Uttar Pradesh.[3] He was the son of a farmer, but was now going to college, majoring in English and economics (he stumbled to answer what his major was when asked by the judges and responded in bad and broken English). There was light-hearted banter and speculation among the judges about his college credentials, but they indulged him, nonetheless, to perform for his audition. He performed an incomprehensible (comical) Bollywood inspired dance routine with utmost earnestness. He said dance was God's gift to him and he had no training. He was eliminated in this round. However, he was one among many thousand more Indians who appear on reality shows who otherwise would never be seen on TV. This was their 15 seconds of fame. The auditions, not unlike the *Dance India Dance* auditions (that I discussed in Chapter 4), were about showing up, being visible, and being counted. Some competed and were excellent dancers, but for many, being on TV was what mattered, even if it was for a few seconds. They occupied a space physically that would not otherwise be theirs, and in doing so thousands of people watched them on screen and they became participants in the culture of celebrity. In the process, they also became citizens of an expanding democracy of a consumerist modernity in India.

In the mix of contestants, there were also sophisticated and glamorous dancers like Karan Pangali from London. He had his own Bollywood dance school. He was well versed in Kathak, Hip-Hop, Jazz, Salsa, and Bollywood dance. His participation in *Just Dance* allowed him to develop a large international following, even though he was eliminated towards

---

[3] The auditions not only showed contestants taking part from remote corners of India but also highlighted the cities where the *Just Dance* crew was travelling. We saw the urban landmarks, the historical sites, the tourist attractions, the food, and throngs of people rushing to meet Hrithik Roshan and signing up for the *Just Dance* auditions. The promotion of *Just Dance* on television was as carefully orchestrated as the dances that were showcased in the show.

the end. I met him at Kadamb Dance Center in Ahmedabad, Kumudini Lakhia's Kathak institute, in 2011. He shared with me many stories about his experience in the show. He said that although he was injured during the show and had a bad infection in his foot, he had very little chance of winning even if he was not injured. He said that the winners were fixed from before and most situations were contrived (this allegation against all reality shows is not new).

Soumita Roy from Kolkata was also a popular contestant who was eliminated towards the end. In fact, she was the only female contestant to remain until the fifth round of this intense competition. Soumita was a student in Rabindra Bharati University in Kolkata, pursuing a master's degree in dance. The daughter of a single mother, Soumita shared with the television audience that she came from a difficult socioeconomic background and had to learn the different dance styles from watching television, as she could not afford teachers. She emerged as a judge's favourite from the very first audition when she danced to the song from the Bollywood film *Guzarish* (starring Hrithik Roshan), 'Ke Tera Zikr Hai' (is it your mention). She displayed her mastery of various Indian classical dance movements by gliding like a peacock, holding her hands in a mudra, leaping, stretching, and lifting her legs elegantly. Soumita called her dance style 'creative' and Vaibhavi Merchant mentioned the famous choreographers in the city of Kolkata, in particular Tanushree Shankar, who was one of the judges for *Naach Dhum Machale*, and who was carrying on the tradition of modern dance developed by Uday Shankar. Soumita also showed her versatility by moving like a contemporary dancer, performing splits, and moving across the dance floor with wide and sweeping movements. The judges declared her outstanding and gave her a special 'star certificate'. Soumita enthralled the judges many more times; an especially memorable episode was her Kathak duet with Karan Pangali dancing to a *tarana* (a north Indian classical musical genre) set to Kathak bols and the melody of 'Ami je tomar' (I am yours) from the film *Bhool Bhulaiyaa* (2007). She was also equally impressive when she partnered with Rajitdev (a contestant from Mumbai) in a Salsa duet to the song 'Bhor Bhaye Panghat Pe' (Dawn breaks along the path to the river) from Hindi film *Satyam Shivam Sundaram* (1978). The original scene had Zeenat Aman carrying a pot and undulating her hips to fetch water from the river (invoking the image of what is known as *panghat lila* among Kathak dancers, and associated with the playful dalliances of Hindu gods Radha and Krishna discussed in Chapter 3). It was obvious from Soumita's dance renditions that the Indian female dancer was no longer only the Radha who carried the pot for panghat lila but carried a cosmopolitan identity that could switch easily from the erotic Salsa dancer to the athletic contemporary dancer to the restrained Indian classical dancer. She was a cosmopolitan hybrid sporting a global dance aesthetic that was not confined to any single ethnic identity.

In sharp contrast to Soumita was Ankan Sen, who had no classical training and was self-trained as a Hip-Hop dancer. Many dancers on reality shows were self-trained, a pattern that must be obvious by now. Even Hrithik Roshan said/claimed during an interview in *Just Dance* that he had no formal training, but had mastered Hip-Hop on his own. Both Ankan and Rajitdev were adept at breaking and popping and their inspirations, they said, were Hrithik Roshan and Michael Jackson.[4] Their intense high-energy dancing rigorously challenged the male identities propagated through classical Indian dances that also articulated

---

[4] Michael Jackson, the king of pop, has been an inspiration for a generation of dancers throughout the world. During my fieldwork, I was astonished to see how Hip-Hop and Break dancing had penetrated all strata of Indian society—from the males at the margins to the Bollywood film stars. The 'Michael Jackson style' of dancing has redefined masculinity in global pop culture and the Indian youth has embraced this identity with full force.

traditional regional identities. The Indian male dancer was not confined to regionally distinct Indian identities anymore. He now displayed a cosmopolitan masculinity derived from the global youth culture of Hip-Hop and Bollywood dances. The rejection of the notions of masculinity embodied in classical and folk dances were sharply expressed during my interviews with male reality show dancers. Some of them simply made fun of classical Indian dances because they thought they were effeminate or had strange facial expressions. The costumes, the songs, and movements were too stylized and old fashioned, and were also difficult to learn, they said.

In the final round of *Just Dance*, the winner of the show Ankan Sen performed a memorable robotic dance where his body, wrapped in silver foil, moved like a machine to electronic music while breaking and popping in Hip-Hop style. He moved like a man-machine (cyborg) across the television screen with blue and green lighting arches and beams in the backdrop. This was the televisual rendering of the mechanized body in postmodern culture. The human-machine hybrid or cyborg dance (a hybrid of dance and televisual technology) has been discussed by dance scholars such as Sherill Dodds (2005) in connection to screen dances. Ankan's exhilarating robotic dance exemplified this complex sensory experience.

The dominance of technological mediation over all other experiences in contemporary global culture has become a subject of great interest for media theorists. Mules (2007) uses the concept of 'phantasmagoria' to describe the dominant form of technological mediation in global culture where the body is immersed in synthetic experiences through an overproduction of visual and tactile images. Mules (2007) calls cyberspace and department stores such phantasmagorias where the outside world is bracketed out and experience is controlled and predetermined. He (Mules 2007) echoes Adorno's view of the mass commodity world that dominates every sphere of our lives today. However, Mules further argues that these technological mediations have enabled the magic of Benjamin's authentic 'aura' to return in a new incarnation through innovative manipulations. The advent of new technology in late capitalism has enabled us to refashion ourselves as products that can be manufactured, manipulated, and controlled. Mules (2007: NP) writes:

We see this phenomenon everywhere in today's 'control societies' in which individuals are encouraged to see themselves as self-directed and self-motivated: free-wheeling consumers and entrepreneurs in a dematerialized world of images and codes. The body is reduced to a techno-organic substance affected directly by manipulating techniques. Aura is reinvested in the body as an immediate experience of 'being connected' where the outside world seemingly dissolves in the presence of a far more enticing virtual world, full of new possibilities for interconnection.

Mules (2007) adds that the material world persists alongside the virtual world, and following his train of thought, I argue that the dancing bodies in reality shows emerge as the ultimate techno-real (objective-subjective) experiences of bodily habituations. The complex sensorium of perceptions experienced as a spectator and a participant of a dance reality show is a new way of being in the world—a world of constant remixing and remediation created through a heightened mode of living expressed through new kinds of affect/emotion and aspiration/ competition aligned with the commodity.

New desires and aspirations moulded through these dance performances on television reality shows produce new disembodied subjectivities in contemporary India. At a more fundamental level, this kind of disembodied subjectivity is connected to 'a crisis of the quotidian' (Wolputte 2004: 260). Accordingly, the habituations and daily routines that gave structure, routine, and continuity to experience are constantly interrupted through travel, information overload, media, or multitasking. Postmodernists call it the crisis of memory. A new kind of fleeting and marketed reality dominates the sensory world of the audience and the performer alike today with the captivating auras of success and celebrity. Dance reality shows are at the heart of these emotional dramas that are simultaneously contrived and real, and in which the pleasures of dancing are transformed into branding and various strategies of winning and losing guided by the promise of transformation. The aesthetic delight of the rasa experience associated with the embodied experience of Indian dances has been transformed into a new kind of euphoria aligned with and inspired by technology, commodity, and celebrity culture.

'Remix' is a techno-physical experience of aesthetic pleasure where corporeality itself is no longer bounded by flesh but is interpenetrated by the machine. Thus, the dancing produces a range of transitory and competing emotions that collapse the past and the present and that do not yet have a discursive configuration. They produce what Appadurai (1997: 30) has eloquently called 'nostalgia without memory'. As production values take center stage in the global circulation of dance, these dance reality shows present to us the entanglement of affect, desire, and eloquent bodies that sway precariously between morality and excessive desire (Chakravorty 2010). The negative association of desire and consumerism is voiced by an Indian citizen in these words (quoted in Ganguly-Scrase and Scrase 2009: 154):

> One of the negative influences of cable is the excessive desire for consumer goods, compared to our time. People are more career-minded, but not necessarily as a result of cable. In the past the capacity to desire something was limited. Our 'chaibar aasha' (capacity to desire) was limited and we asked for very little and our eagerness for wanting things was limited. Now even 10–12 year olds constantly want this and that. Their eagerness to want things is immense.

Digitized Desires in Everyday Life

Now I delve deeper into the lives of a few dancers and choreographer from *Naach Dhum Machale* to articulate their individual desires, struggles, and dance experiences in reality shows. I show how their embodiment as a reality show dancer is integrated with their everyday lives. I followed these dancers intermittently from 2006 to 2011; I visited their dance classes (some are described in the previous chapter), their homes, met them in shopping malls, and chatted with them over coffee. In the process, I learned about their zigzagging careers in the reality show world, their passion for dance, their strengths and disappointments. Through these brief and incomplete fragments of their lives, I hope to present their voices as they eke out a living through dance in contemporary India. I try to show how they express their subjectivities, the choices they have made to participate in the reality show world, their cultivation of cosmopolitanism, their negotiation of the global forces of media and market, their role as cultural entrepreneurs from relatively marginal contexts, their unpredictable and improvisational lifestyles, and above all their agency.

Bhaskar

I have come up from the grassroots. I have lived in *tali* houses [houses that have fragile tiled rather than solid concrete roofs]. Now I live in a mess house here [a mess house is a sort of non-collegiate dormitory]. *Mati kamre pore achhi* (I am biting the ground to survive). My family is originally from Bihar, from Chhapra district. I grew up in Beharampur in Bengal with five brothers and sisters. My father was a make-up artist and a theatre worker. He did plays with Harijans (the lowest caste in the hierarchy of caste, or outside it, better categorized as Dalits) in Beharampur; his group was called Harijan Natya Sanstha. I used to accompany him for 12 years doing make-up and participating in the plays. Then about 18 or 19 years ago, Saswata Roy came to perform. He did not use any music, just played the radio and danced. He did what is called *Jibanmukhi naach* (life-oriented dance) through experimenting with movements from Hip-Hop. He learned break dancing by watching Michael Jackson videos.

He died very young in a motorcycle accident. I started break dancing and would practice on my own. Before that, I thought dance was only for girls, I never thought I would dance. I graduated with a degree in philosophy from a local university. I had entered the university through the Scheduled Caste quota. I had no opportunities, so I came to Kolkata to enroll in Rabindra Bharati University in 2006 for a master's degree. I came because I got Rs 1,200 as stipend from the university. I was introduced to Bharatanatyam, I mean proper Bharatanatyam there. Where I come from people don't get the opportunity to learn proper technique. They usually learn from a guru's student of a student of a student. The form is diluted and you end up learning the wrong technique. I learned Bharatanatyam from Rabindra Burman, who took a lot of interest in me and trained me without a fee. He said my base was strong and I could learn the dance well. I studied Kalari with Roger Sinha from Kerala Kalamandalam. I have also done workshops with the most eminent modern dancer in India, Astad Deboo.

After graduating from Rabindra Bharati, I did not know what to do with my life. I became frustrated. I started working at ICICI Prudential as a salesman travelling all over India. After six months, I quit. There were 36 people doing the same thing in my office and I knew I was different. I have been dancing for 18 years. I started dancing with Sapphire Creations, the contemporary dance company in Kolkata. I started doing contemporary and modern dance there. They used to give me some money for dancing. My family, of course, could not support my decision or me. I had many brothers and sisters, a lot of responsibility. Then I got a chance to participate in *Naach Dhum Machale* on ETV Bangla. It was a great opportunity. However, I was asked to choreograph on dancers in that show, some of whom had no base in dance. That is why I could not reach the finals of the show. I reached until the top four but could not get to the finals. But I was able to show my knowledge and creativity in the show. I choreographed Bharatanatyam *adavu's* (basic positions, movements, gestures) lying on the floor in one of the pieces. About a hundred students graduated with me from Rabindra Bharati university in dance, but how many were able to get work in this profession. I got work because I could do a variety of dance styles.

I work nationally as well as internationally. Most choreographers just copy choreography from Bollywood films. I do not like to copy. I like to listen to the music first. Then I think of what kind of movements inspire me to move with the music. I have a strong visual sense. During *Nach Dhum Machale,* Ringo-Da (who is a film director and was a judge on the show) spoke about presentation, grooming, and visual appeal. Reality shows are a tough world. You need body training, regular exercises, and a lot of stamina. In local reality shows such as *Naach Dhum Machale* there is not much editing for the dancing. There is only one take. So you have to do everything right the first time. Sometimes we rehearsed for the entire night; we started rehearsing at 1:30 am some nights and rehearsed until 8:00 am. We did not sleep for more than two hours for days during the show. We just gulped a lot of Red Bull. There is a lot of pressure from production to do things quickly, as these shows (with small budgets) are not shot for an extended amount of time.

If you cannot do it or the money is too low for you, someone else will be hired. We were paid only Rs 1,500 per choreography in *Naach Dhum Machale.* There are many like me in Kolkata now. However, many just dance for a short time, until their entry into the film world or TV serial world. But I want to stick to dance and choreography. I would like to do more stage shows. Here we are paid Rs 10,000 for stage shows. I would like to go to Bombay to do work. I have done choreography for the hit show *Dance India Dance* in Bombay. I went with a dancer called Aditi from here. There were famous Bollywood judges in the show like Saroj Khan, Vaibhavi Merchant, and Terence Lewis. You need a lot of lobby in Bombay to get work. I am getting some work to do choreography in Bengali films. It is keeping me busy, but I am not training or experimenting with my art. I cannot be creative when I work in films, they are all formulaic choreography. Choreographers like Sajid (who was also in *Naach Dhum Machale* and then in *Dance Bangla Dance*) just copy moves from Bollywood films. I like to create my own style and experiment and improve. My only income is from dance so I have to take all the work I get. I am currently working for the television channel Star Jalsha in a program where I am getting paid Rs 2,500 per choreography. I am able to show my creativity in this show. I like to teach kids; with them, you can be truly creative. I make them work hard with their bodies. I play some music and ask them to close their eyes. I make them move around with eyes closed and make patterns with their hands.

My hero is Prabhu Deva (a Bollywood actor, dancer, and choreographer). He is unique in his innovations of Hip-Hop. He choreographed the song 'Main Aisa Kyun Hoon' (Why I am like this? from the film *Lakhsya*, 2004) by using hand *mudras* (gestures) from classical dance in a Hip-Hop fusion. I do think you should have an Indian dance base even if you do contemporary or western dance. Now, everybody wants western dance, nobody wants to learn Indian classical or folk. You will see on the street corners and alleyways where they used to have advertisements for classical Indian or folk classes, now they have western, salsa, jazz, and Bollywood. Nobody really cares about the proper technique of these styles, if you say you teach these styles then students will sign up. The quality does not matter. Who is going to judge authenticity? Audiences do not know, they just want to see the glitter and the lights. The reality shows are making things easy, everything is packaged. People just want to show their faces on TV. The dancers are training for six months. The audience likes to see emotional drama; these reality shows are whipping up the drama through dance competition. You see, they are in the business of selling emotions. The more emotional dramas you create, more the product sells. In this case the reality shows sell the dances and the products they advertise. The good thing about these shows is that people are getting some work, and for at least 10 bad dances, we do see one good one.

When I was growing up the names of modern dance choreographers we heard were Tanushree Shankar and Manjushree Chaki-Sircar who were from the educated elite class, but now the young ones hear names such as Terence Lewis and Farah Khan. They are all Bollywood choreographers and that is who has status. I have a plan for a reality show; I have proposed it to Star TV. I want to make a journey with a group of dancers to different states of India, learn different folk styles as a group, and present these styles in a reality show format. We will teach about our own folks styles that are disappearing, train our bodies to absorb the culture and the movement before they disappear completely.

Sajid Jamal

I had a small business of selling caps in Park Circus, Kolkata, before I participated in reality shows. My mother is a seamstress, so I used to make and sell caps. We are three brothers. My youngest sibling is a carom champion; my eldest sibling is a promoter. I am in the middle and I wanted to dance. My parents did not encourage me. But I dropped out of school in class ten. I am self-trained. I learned Break and Hip-Hop by watching Michael Jackson videos. One of my relatives, who is a homeopathy doctor, recognized my talent and suggested I join reality shows. Now I am successful. I have my own place, I have decorated it, I bought a bike, and I feel I am on my way. I had no one backing me. I have made it on my own. But still you see, dancing is not OK. For rich people they go swimming and play basketball games, for people like me, we dance on reality shows. I started in *Jhum Tara Ra Ra* and because Rimjhim, the dancer for whom I choreographed came second (this show had one dancer for one choreographer), I was noticed. I started getting a lot of work. I perform Contemporary, Hip-Hop, Bollywood, and Western; and because these are in demand, I am busy. If you have talent, then reality show is a forum where this talent will come out. I have struggled for a long time. I am still struggling, but now everybody in Kolkata knows me. Sometimes, there is talk about my being Muslim, but generally, I get work (see Figure 5.2).

My performing group consists of eight dancers who are paid for their performances. We get Rs 15,000 per show. But that includes transport and costumes. The competition is fierce. Someone might do a show for Rs 10,000 and then we have to do it for that amount. We sometimes get eight shows per month, sometimes six, sometimes none. So, we just have to do all the shows we get. Sometimes we dance even with

FIGURE 5.2   Sajid Jamal, Choreographer, Kolkata
Source: Author.

injuries because we never know what is coming next month and what if there are no shows! My other income is from training kids in a class in Kabardanga. I charge them Rs 400 a month. I give discount to poor people. Sometimes if they cannot pay I say it is fine. I am now opening a studio in Sodpur and one in Jamshedpur. The Jamshedpur studio is part of Saroj Khan Academy (Saroj Khan is a famous Bollywood choreographer). She will come there once a year. But the people there know me from television, they wanted me to come and teach. The *puja* season (the Bengali festive season in autumn) is great for shows. We just did a show for the famous Bollywood singer Udit Narayan with my professional team. My professional team practices in my studio in Chandni. We will be travelling to Singapore as part of Udit Narayan's team. We have to get passports and visa for everyone. We are very excited to travel outside India. We are also performing at Science City here for the 'Kalakar Awards'. We are also travelling to Bokaro for a show where they will pay Rs 20,000. The show will launch a product ...'a beverage'. We have to provide the 'item girl' and the 'item boy' for the show. After paying my dancers Rs 1,000–2,000, there is not much left for me. But still it is great ... *dance ko leke jeena hai* (I want to live life with dance).

I had gone to Mumbai as a backup dancer before I participated in the reality shows *Jhum Tara Nara* and *Dance Dhum Machale*. I gave up backup dancing because I wanted to be a choreographer, to strike out on my own. The reality shows helped me a lot to establish my career. But there is too much politics in the reality shows. These shows sometimes have everything decided from before and the winner is fixed. They manipulate the situation by giving the choreographers songs that are difficult to choreograph. They give the best song to the choreographer they want to see win. Reality show is a business. I can also produce a reality show if I have the money. All I have to do is book a channel and produce a show. It is all about the TRP. But I am interested in doing good work.

I am keen on doing choreography for 'item numbers'. *Mera pehchan reality show se hua, phirbhi hamara kuch alag se kam, alag se dance shows ke liye koshish hai* (I became known through reality shows, but I want to try different kinds of dance, different kinds of shows now). We also do corporate shows and charity shows. Now, I need to make my own dance institute, I need some space to own. I am renting these spaces for my classes and rehearsals and they keep increasing the rent. It's getting very expensive. I have many students now coming to me from long distances. Many people come to follow their dream in reality shows. They may be college dropouts, but they want to be a star. They want to dance like an 'item girl' or an 'item boy'. They also want to become choreographers. Then someday may be a celebrity. My student numbers are growing and there is a future for me.

Sanjukta

I have loved dancing since I have been a small child. But being from an ordinary Bengali middle-class family this was not taken very seriously. I started serious training with Mamata Shankar Ballet group when I was older. I was with them for nine years. Then I started classes with Odissi exponent Sutapa Talukdar and I trained for six years. My foundation in classical Odissi is strong; I have even received the Sanjukta Panigrahi award. I also did workshops on the folk style Purulia Chhauu. I saw Russian ballet and gymnastics on TV and wanted to learn those styles as well. I was so enamored that I started practicing gymnastics on my own. Unfortunately, I have never learned western dance in a proper way. I was studying dance in Rabindra Bharati University when someone I know wanted me to audition for the reality show *Naach Dhum Machale* in 2005. In Rabindra Bharati University, I was one of the first to enter a reality show competition. There was a lot of controversy among the professors surrounding my decision as they look down upon reality shows.

I was selected and the grooming sessions started. The group was trained how to dress, walk, improvise with music, and so on. We were trained how to perform in front of a camera. We were asked to show a lot of emotion ... that seemed to me more like acting than actual dancing or expressing dance-related emotions. There were 10 cameras shooting us during the actual performance rounds. We were assigned choreographers. The choreographers gave us instructions about costume and jewellery. I met Sajid-da (Sajid Jamal) on the sets of *Naach Dhum Machale*. I liked his performance and began training in break dance from him. You need a lot of stamina for reality shows. We used to do six shoots in one day, without any breaks. Sometimes in three days we had to prepare and perform seven dances. We rehearsed for entire days and nights. I won the competition.

In the reality show *Nach Baliye* on Star Plus, they were looking for a *baliye*, a female dancing partner for the television actor Harshad Chopra. It was called *Talash-e-Baliye*. The show was about celebrity couple dancing. I won. This was a huge exposure for me on national TV. The auditions were conducted all over India, in cities of Bombay, Delhi, Kolkata, Lucknow, and others. Four hundred dancers participated from Kolkata alone. The years 2008 and 2009 were very memorable for me. My mother had accompanied me to Bombay. I was there for 12 days. The industry people took care of my transportation and hotel costs. There was no winner's award, though. I performed with Harshad Chopra in the grand finale to the item song 'Zara Zara Touch Me' from the Bollywood film *Race* (2008). The choreography was easy because Harshad is not really a dancer but a celebrity. Everything was very professional in Bombay. There was a lot of respect for maintaining time. We were always sent home after the choreography was completed. There was no waiting for hours without proper schedules, like in Kolkata. This was a big budget affair, unlike Kolkata. The choreography was also crisp. We had to keep rehearsing until the choreography and movement were perfect. Bollywood stars like Shahrukh Khan and Lara Dutta were the judges and guests for the show.

But after this big exposure to glamour and the limelight, I did not get work. I have not really understood this reality show world. The next season of *Nach Baliye* did not happen. After winning this competition my life has not been very good. I went into a deep depression. I was not called for award ceremonies in Star Plus to participate as a dancer, the industry people just turned away from me. Although they had told me earlier that because of my dancing their TRPs had gone up, they did not call me for any of their shows. This kind of sudden exposure from reality shows can be misleading. They also push people from humble backgrounds to show the world that they are supporting talent. This is how they gain sympathy from the audience and their TRP shoots up. Maybe I did not fit the model. I was also asked to go for audition in *Dance India Dance* and *Just Dance,* but I did not want to participate in reality shows anymore. I did not go.

But, even in the classical world I was not selected, despite my recognition and awards. In the classical world there is very little money. People spend their own money to do shows. There were many kinds of politics in the government. For instance in Indian Council for Cultural Relations (ICCR) there is politics about which artists are selected for touring abroad or getting sponsors. I have sent them a letter to be an empanelled classical Odissi artist.

I was asked to do a few television serials; one was a serial on *Devi Chaudhurani,* a novel written by Bankim Chandra Chattopadhyay. But it did not materialize, ultimately the production house changed. I am not interested in becoming a television serial actor. I want to be a full-time dancer and a choreographer and for this I will need time to practice and hone my artistic skills. Television serial acting will not leave any time for me to do the dance practice. So I have rejected that path. Interestingly, I had a lot of trouble with the television industry, yet many dancers who are chosen from small towns like Durgapur or Arambagh come and thrive in the city (Kolkata) and in the industry. There is also the problem of the casting couch. I do not want to get into those kinds of compromises. But these days, the dancers want to become stars. They already have Facebook celebrity pages; celebrities have touched them so they too are celebrities. Many will do anything to get ahead.

What I am doing now is what I would have done even if I had not been a reality show champion. I have started a dance group with some friends. I am also teaching children in my home. I am studying about dance on my own. The dance reality shows did give me some exposure; like my neighbours know about my dancing now. I was able to travel to the U.K. to perform for Sampad. My wish is to invent a new form of dance style. I want to create contemporary choreographies like the acclaimed choreographer Daksha Seth. We also have dancers like Alokananda Roy and Tanushree Shankar doing modern dance in Kolkata. There are accomplished classical dancers in the city like Sharmila Biswas, Sutapa Roy, Aloka Kanungo (all trained in the Odissi style). They are classically trained, but they are innovating and are doing new things.

Reality shows give you the chance to perform in front of the public very quickly. Even before you can develop any style or skill. But I am not interested anymore. The dancers in the reality shows use the platform to break into films to perform 'item numbers'. I know some who are doing that in Bengali films. But I have no intention of joining films. The reality shows or film dancing will not give me the choice to select my own choreographer, costume, music, and jewellery. I was asked to wear these low cut dresses during the reality shows, I was not comfortable, I complained, and they put a net on them. It felt ridiculous.

I am happy teaching my own students in my home. I have 15–16 now. But I will grow the numbers. I have just started. There are many talented dancers in Kolkata. They do not want to perform 'item numbers', but the choices are shrinking. Who will give them a platform? I want to take a chance and stick to my own teaching and creative work. I have planned to do some work with Bhaskar-da (Bhaskar Raut) who is also on reality shows (Figure 5.3). He is a very good dancer. We are thinking of creating a piece and touring.

This chapter has shown how the arrival of cable and satellite networks created a paradigm shift in the narratives of national identity and modernity in India that had been perpetuated through the state-owned network, Doordarshan. The liberalization of the market and the arrival of cable networks ushered in a new kind of television programming among which dance competitions such as *Foot Loose* and *Boogie Woogie* became a thriving presence. These shows challenged the propagation of classical Indian dances on national programs on Doordarshan and gradually the audience turned away from such programming. As more and more dance and music competitions came to dominate the television

FIGURE 5.3   Choreographers Remo De Souza and Bhaskar Raut
Source: Author.

networks, Bollywood songs and dances became the major source of the programming. Now, the dance reality shows (among other forms of reality shows) have exploded on the television networks. These shows display a variety of dance or musical styles that use the aesthetics of 'remix' packaged in the form of 'item numbers' for a national and global Indian audience.

The traditional identities of femininity and masculinity associated with Indian dances are diffused in a media-saturated world where the 'remix' genres now dominate. These new kinds of global dances of Salsa, Hip-Hop, Bollywood, Kathak, Contemporary, and Bharatanatyam produce new cosmopolitan Indian identities. These experiences of dance produce a new kind of media-embodiment and inter-cultural/inter-sensory mobile subjectivity that is in a perpetual state of flux. But the labour of the corporeal body in dance persists despite such media driven phantasmagoria. The bodies sweat it out in dance studios, in classes, and in everyday lives. As our perceptual faculties are reshaped by the commercially driven aesthetics of 'remix' and manipulated by a virtual world of images and codes where our desires appear to be hermeneutically sealed and packaged, 'real' dancers from various walks of life struggle to survive as economic agents and strive for creative freedom to become artists.

6

A Struggle for Identity

India is currently going through one of its most turbulent phases of transformation. Political corruption is at its worst, crony-capitalism threatens to destroy the very fabric of democracy and religio-political vested interests are coercing the common citizen to polarize. Created by the web of these daunting trends is a deep and growing cultural trauma of an India that is arguably alienating itself from a syncretic, modern and dynamic 5,000-year-old civilization to becoming an unrecognizable, imitative, regressive society, nay, market. (Ramanathan 2010)

Many educated Indians today feel new anxieties and desperations. Sharada, a respected film director and cultural critic, seems to confirm those feelings while making an affirmation of the cultural values of the *Margazhi* Festival in Chennai, which, she claims, remains uncorrupted by the market. Since the early 1990s, the liberal economy in India has ushered in many kinds of transformations in the public sphere. Some of the key elements of these changes have been theorized under the framework of 'media and globalization' in academic disciplines like anthropology in which the core argument is that the growth and globalization of the media have precipitated dramatic aesthetic and structural changes in the cultural sphere. My focus in this book has been more specific—on the bodily practices of dance and the sweeping changes that came over it due to the new media, the aesthetics of 'remix', and consumerism. The combination of these resulted in the merging and collision of 'low' and 'high' cultures. I looked at how these changes in the practice and circulation of dance created new kinds of affect, pedagogy, and economic opportunity; new and controversial ideals of femininity and masculinity, and a new global culture of a cosmopolitan Indian identity.

The new media and the prominence of Bollywood created a new awareness and popularity of Indian dances. The audience for dance was enlarged and, as a result, new and exciting opportunities opened up for the emergent classes and generations who could now dream of pursuing careers as dancers and choreographers; careers that were previously mostly reserved for the educated elite or hereditary practitioners (this was certainly the case in the classical dance culture). As dance reality shows exploded on television, dance studios, and dance spaces mushroomed in cities such as Kolkata and Mumbai to accommodate the demands of a new generation of dancers. I followed a few dancers and choreographers in various ethnographic contexts to represent this urban youth culture of dreams, struggles, and possibilities in the preceding pages.

It is necessary to remember, however, that the liberalization of the Indian economy is a polarizing issue; it is associated with many accounts of upward mobility of the lower middle and working classes in contemporary India, but at the same time, some argue that it created even greater class/caste divides. Though controversial and often exploitative, the Bollywood and reality show world is a slice of this polarized narrative of class mobility and visibility of an aspirational generation. The performers are not part of the information technology (IT) industry, the retail industry, or the call centers of a liberalized economy, but they are perhaps the most visible, yet understudied, group in the accounts of a new India.

This concluding chapter reflects on the heated debates around the complex transition of Indian culture from a Nehruvian socialist economy to a liberalizing and globalizing economy. Dance reality shows open up both the public and private cultural battlegrounds of this structural transformation. As the nation delves deeper into the messiness of markets and questions of democracy and modernity, a powerful message seems to radiate from the screens of dance reality shows, that can simply be summarized as: 'We all want to be modern and be counted.' Here being modern translates as gaining the status of historical actors who can no longer be denied temporal coexistence with the middle and upper classes in India and be homogenized as the unwashed masses, needing to be educated and civilized. In short, no longer to be confined in the 'waiting room of history' as they demand full participation in the cultural life of the nation.[1] Yet, this is a message that is not clearly heard, or, if heard, not well-received by many, including the elite gatekeepers of Indian 'culture'. In the first section that follows, titled 'Everybody Wants to Be Modern', I look at this dimension of dance reality shows: as a site for class mobility and democracy, but also as a site for anxieties and threats generated by this new social order. These shows blatantly challenge the older norms and aesthetics of dancing associated with traditional middle-class values and gender identities.[2] The second section titled 'Morality and Corruption', focuses on the discursive debates

---

[1] The idea of the 'imaginary waiting room of history' is associated with the critique of historicism by Dipesh Chakrabarty in the context of decolonization and historical consciousness, and brings up the central question regarding political modernity in the non-Western societies (Chakrabarty 2000: 8–9; also mentioned Baviskar and Ray 2011 as 'the waiting room of modernity').

[2] I will not go into the debate of whether liberalization simultaneously also reproduces the older structures of inequalities of caste, religion, gender, and class, as argued by some scholars as it is not relevant here. See Fernandes (2011) for a discussion.

regarding reality shows, and the lure of fame and the stigma of corruption that continues to trouble middle-class morality. It also reflects on the grave dangers lurking in the right wing moral rhetoric of cultural pollution associated with the current national government in Delhi. The third section, 'Sexual Politics and Dance Desires', looks specifically at ordinary women and their aspirations and negotiations to claim a modern respectable identity through commercial dance platforms such as the dance reality shows.

Everybody Wants to Be Modern

As high and low culture merge due to liberalization and produce remixed cultural products such as dance reality shows, it also produces new forms of affect and identity-markers for entry into the middle classes. These identity markers are by no means monolithic, just as the term 'modern' itself is not unidimensional, and are closer to the ideals of multiplicity and post-modernity. Sheth (1999, quoted in Baviskar and Ray 2011) observes:

> Liberalization promises the pleasures of the market—a cornucopia of commodities magical and sensuous—as a hedonistic supplement to an older-middle class concern with maintaining social distance. To be part of the middle class is to express oneself through consumption, and to establish one's identity as being distinct from the lower classes through a set of cultural markers that proclaim one's 'good taste' and style.

What is 'good taste and style' in contemporary India, especially concerning practices of the body, such as the art of dancing? What marks the category of aesthetic citizenship? The older cultural markers of 'good taste' associated with the classical/traditional performing arts (that evoked a civilizational lineage and historicity) are now unsettled and flattened out due to the new media and the democratization of taste. The avant-garde dance artists who are associated with 'contemporizing'

Indian classical dances are a small cross-section of the super elite (who mostly continue to create their lineage through the classical arts) and are not relevant here (see Katrak 2011 for a discussion on Contemporary dance in India and the diaspora). The term 'contemporary dance' itself, I posit, can be understood as plural. It is amorphous and the reality show dancers use their own versions of contemporary dance; the category/ term itself is up for grabs. This is not unlike how both groups—the avant-garde and reality show dancers—use the term 'modern dance', which has some elements of the Euro-American dance vocabularies and/or choreographic conventions but is open to interpretations.

I argue that the dance reality shows and Bollywood dances are distinct cultural practices in urban India that produce new markers of prestige and taste. But they are controversial and full of erotic and captivating desires that provoke and disturb the middle-class perception of good taste. For instance, debates about the blatant commercialization and vulgarization of Indian culture and history through 'item numbers' resurfaced recently surrounding the film *Bajirao Mastani* (2015). The Non-govenmental organization, Bharat Against Corruption (that is aligned with the Bhartiya Janata Party [BJP]) wanted to ban the song 'Pinga', which is a Lavani (a Maharashtrian folk dance) inspired 'item number' danced by Bollywood stars Deepika Padukone and Priyanka Chopra. Bharat Against Corruption considered it obscene and vulgar and a distortion of history. The 'item number' was a big hit and acquired a large audience following and became a popular dance number in reality shows. At the other end of the ideological spectrum, the veteran Bollywood actress Shabana Azmi, who self-identifies as a social activist, has been critical of 'item numbers' as sanctioned products of the male gaze to objectify women's bodies. In a recent show on NDTV sponsored by L'Oréal (celebrating International Women's Day) she pointed to the lyrics of the hit item song 'Main to Tandoori Murgi Hoon Yaar, Gatkaale Saiyyan Alcohol Se' (I am a tandoori chicken, lover, gobble me with alcohol) as an example of the perpetuation of this kind of attitude in society. She argued that although the number was written and composed and sponsored by a few, it was seen by crores of Indians. She added that women have no autonomy on how the camera captures their bodies and that there should be self-regulation about such representation rather than allowing the morality brigade to do so. Ravish Kumar, the journalist hosting the show, added that young children dance to these lyrics in schools every day, normalizing such sexualized portrayals of women. If we take the long view, however, and we should, we recall that, among other things, it was the sexually explicit lyrics in devadasi and tawaif performances that affronted women reformers such as Rukmini Devi and others who 'cleaned up' and 'purified' the forms and made them 'classical' and oriented to worship and the divine.

I propose that it is this knotted dialectic between the construction of middle class taste / value and the desire to be modern that is at the core of the aesthetic transformation of dance in India. Therefore, desire and subjectivity intertwine in unique ways for this quest for postcolonial modernity. Despite the fact that Bollywood dance has broken through its prior 'low culture' status due to factors such as its association with glamorous figures like Shiamak Davar and its popularity among the diaspora and demand in weddings (especially the once-regional now pan-Indian 'ritual' of 'sangeet' in the moneyed class), I argue that its artistic value remains questionable among cultural pundits.[3] The desire to be modern was previously anchored in the values of tradition and nation, but under liberalization and globalization it is anchored in the market, consumption, and branding.[4]

[3] See Morcom (2013) for a discussion on the embourgeoisement of Bollywood dance and Ganti (2012) on Bollywood in terms of gentrification.

[4] I have explored the intersections of tradition or invented tradition and modernity in Chakravorty (2008).

In my earlier work on the classical Indian dance, Kathak, and its democratization, I had argued that knowledge of the classical dances functioned as a form of cultural capital in shaping an ideal national/ Indian identity among the middle and lower middle classes (Chakravorty 2008). But in the post-liberalization era, tradition and classicism are no longer seen unquestioningly as 'modern' or 'civilizational' (in fact, they are often associated with feudal vestiges of the past) and are being overhauled as forces of globalization and pop culture shaping new cosmopolitan Indian subjects. This does not mean, by any means, that classical Indian dances have disappeared, but only that they now have to compete with Bollywood and other hybrid and western styles. The new generation of dancers and dance-makers has placed the fusion of various dance styles at the center of their identity formation. The aesthetic of 'remix' has produced intercultural and intertextual bodies that are versatile and global and not confined to any particular tradition or aesthetic. Bollywood dance practice and its derivative versions displayed in the reality show genre are potent engines for producing these new kinds of hybrid consumerist identities.

The dance reality shows have successfully forged a powerful association with an urban modern identity and celebrity culture. These values have fostered a sense of hope and belonging among the upwardly mobile working classes and middle classes to gain social status. The 'middle class' itself is not a homogenous category (neither is the notion of 'modern'). It is internally fractured with regional differences and differing attitudes to Indianness, globalization, and westernization. But one could argue that the surge from below to participate in media practices has opened up Bollywood and other forms of dance as pathways to economic sustenance and some forms of mobility. At a minimum, media artifacts such as reality shows are the new roads not only to celebrity-hood but also to simple relevance. For example, the popular reality show *Sa Re Ga Ma Pa* on Zee Bangla has launched a novel reality show on folk music (accompanied by dancing) by traditional musicians from rural Bengal. This can be interpreted as a serious intervention in the cultural sphere to sustain folk traditions and offer an alternative to Bollywood culture. However, at the same time, the show and the musicians have all been packaged according to the trappings of the market and commodity aesthetics. They are required to uphold the ideology of 'presentability' (discussed in Chapter 4) despite such interventionist intensions. McLuhanites would argue here that what the audience responds to is not the content but the medium through which it is conveyed; in short, the medium is the message and the rural musicians will have to be moulded according to the dictates of reality TV and thus considered modern.

Consider a different dimension of morality/taste and modern identity: gender identity. The proliferation of the 'item girls' and 'item boys' as symbols of the new femininity and masculinity in India has forcefully challenged the earlier constructions of *Bhadramahila* (respectable women) and *Bhadralok* (respectable men). Although those older terms arose from qualities ascribed to Bengali middle-class respectability during Indian nationalism, they had a pan-Indian significance (Chatterjee 1989; Sinha 2014). The marking of femininity and masculinity through the youthful and overly sexualized identities of 'item girls' and 'item boys' has opened up new debates about gatekeeping, morality, and Indianness. For instance, the recent hype about an advertisement for Lux soap where Shahrukh Khan soaks in the bath tub with flower petals floating about and soaps himself luxuriantly while surrounded by a bevy of Bollywood beauties has sent a strong message regarding the reconstruction of masculinity and gender stereotypes in India (for an elaboration see Dasgupta and Gokulsing 2015). The new construction of masculinity through 'item boys' contributes to this ongoing complicated reconstruction of Indian masculinity. Indian dance in general and dance reality shows in particular enrich these insights on gender stereotypes as I show through my ethnography in Mumbai and Kolkata.

The powerful influences of Bollywood dance in shaping gender identity, especially young women and their everyday practices and conduct have penetrated various cross-sections of society including Muslim lower class girls in *bastis* (slums) in Kolkata, writes Kobita Chakraborty (2015). Through Bollywood dancing these young girls from conservative backgrounds are exploring premarital romance and transgressing societal norms and expectations. But contradictory messages abound. For instance, new celebrations of bejeweled women and domesticity (with the excesses of Bollywood aesthetics found in movies such as *Devdas* 2002) find a new recasting in soap operas that are regularly shown on TV. The popularity of soap operas such as *Kahani Ghar Ghar Ki* (The Story of Every Home) and *Kyunki Saas Bhi Kabhi Bahu Thi* (Because Even Mother-in-law Was Once a Daughter-in-Law) are examples of such household melodramas (Fazal 2009: 48–9). Mankekar (1999) has analysed the recasting of the new Indian women in television serials where she is represented as modern, educated, Hindu, and part of the aspiring middle-classes.[5]

Such debates on gender identity often paint liberalization as unleashing unbridled desire, consumerism, and westernization. As Mazzarella observes (2003, quoted in Baviskar and Ray 2011: 21):

> Liberalization promises a mode of citizenship grounded in sensuous resonance; its affect-saturated images and sounds hover between sanctioned desire and the pornography of fetishized commodities. Policing the play of desires in this public sphere is infinitely harder; hence, these desires (and the anxieties about their transgression) get displaced to the 'safe zone' of cinema censorship.

[5] Recent scholarly works on gender, media, and popular culture have comparatively analysed the representations of women in soap operas and TV serials in pre- and post-liberalization India. Many of these scholars argue that the new representations, especially after liberalization, are often antithetical to feminist sensibilities (Fazal 2009; Dasgupta et al. 2011).

Although Mazzarella is referring to cinema censorship here, dance reality shows and reality shows in general have also been subject to moral scrutiny and censorship. The censorship of dance is of course not new in India. The controversies and censorship on dance have spanned from the colonial and nationalist discourses and policies of the 'anti-nautch movement' to the recent ban on bar dancers in Mumbai. However, dance reality shows are a double-edged sword as they are part both of the powerful and excessive culture of desire and consumption and are avenues for 'real' possibilities of human agency and democracy.

Morality and Corruption

The national discourse about the irrepressible power of dance reality shows to corrupt the morals of the entire country, especially the middle classes, surfaced during an episode of *Naach Dhum Machale*, when Shinjini, a 16-year-old contestant from Kolkata, a student in a 'respectable' school, collapsed during the show due to a sudden attack of paralysis. Her limbs and vocal chords were paralyzed and some experts said it was a psycho-somatic attack caused by intense stress. Another reality show participant submerged himself in water on stage and fell unconscious. He was only 23 years old. The audiences were aghast to see how much these children and young adults were willing to endure for their brief dalliance with fame. More shocking, perhaps, was the parental ambition in pushing these young minds and bodies to the point of making them victims of the television industry. An industry, that we know, cares only about its TRPs. The *Indian Express* (16 July 2008) ran a story thus:

> They'll sing, they'll dance, they'll even risk their lives just for their fifteen minutes in the limelight. Reality TV makes everyone a star, and perhaps, everyone a victim of television programming gone bad.

The Kolkata-based English daily newspaper *The Telegraph* had this to say after Shinjini collapsed (Raha 2008):

Last week, the Union minister for women and child development, Renuka Chowdhury, announced that the government would bring in guidelines to regulate Reality Shows for children. It would also introduce a code of conduct for the judges who are sometimes shockingly harsh on the participants. This is heartening news, for it is indeed time that the government stepped in to monitor this modern-day gladiatorial combat with children as the combatants.

However, censorship or regulation of children's participation in reality shows never came through as shows like *Dance Bangla Dance*, one of the most successful shows on Bengali television, even now has children as young as six gyrating to spicy Bollywood numbers. In fact, a new dance reality show for kids was launched in 2016 titled *Super Dancer* with Bollywood actress Shilpa Shetty as the celebrity judge.

The confluence of consumerism, eroticization, and celebrity culture through dance and music form a delectable form of desire that is on display on dance reality shows. The middle-class anxieties surrounding dance reality shows arise at least partially from this allure of the senses and the power of fame and social mobility. There is a real possibility, even danger, that such anxieties will be appropriated by the censorship discourse that is now emerging from the Hindu right wing government in India and states like Maharashtra about the purity of Indian culture. The addition of ultra-Hindu nationalist zeal to liberalization and globalization provides a new kind of twist to the discourses of both liberalization and censorship in India. This particular discourse is far more lethal than the class ambivalences associated with discourses of morality and consumerist modernity that have been prevalent so far. Here is an example (Sumi 2015):

During a meeting with leaders of the Rashtriya Swayamsevak Sangh (RSS) last week, the Union culture and human resource development ministers pledged to launch a countrywide movement to rid the nation of '*sanskritik pradushan* (cultural pollution),' it has emerged now. We will cleanse every area of public discourse that has been westernised and where Indian culture and civilisation need to be restored.

This is an ominous signal for all cultural practices in India and opens a censorship discourse that flies in the face of liberalization and globalization—which can just as easily be read as openness and pluralism—that have been reshaping India's public sphere since the 1990s. Dancing is a fundamental right, just like eating, and what and how people eat or dance cannot be a domain for the state to exercise its 'moral authority' but remains an arena for the expression of personal habits, tastes, and preferences. But the debates surrounding the 'excessive' desire that is on display in dance reality shows and the anxieties regarding women's sexuality continue to spill over the screen into public and private spaces.

Sexual Politics and Dance Desires

Dance reality shows open up new anxieties and debates about desire, consumerism, morality, and sexuality that impact on middle-class sensibilities. Much like during an earlier period of nationalist discourse, women's bodies are important sites of these contestations, and dance reality shows such as *Dhum Machale* are public battlegrounds for young women and their mothers. Although, many young women use these shows to claim a new modern urban identity that is no longer bounded by the nationalist construction of respectable women, they often face middle class and upper middle class disdain. It is interesting to note that while the nationalist construction of Indian women as repositories of tradition and spiritual identity (goddess/*devi*/mother) is being turned on its head by a new generation of women and men in India, who are engaged in redefining femininity and masculinity through bodily dispositions that are cosmopolitan and global in their orientation, there a lingering preoccupation with mother and goddess/devi, especially among the political class.[6]

These paradoxes and anxieties are often expressed by reality show contestants as they navigate the real world of dance 'reality shows'. I once talked with a reality show contestant in her modest living room in a not-so-fashionable part of South Kolkata. She was one of the youngest contestants in that show (who were usually between 18 and 30). Dressed in a miniskirt and with highlighted hair, she looked motivated, well groomed, trendy, and vulnerable. Her mother came in during our conversation with tea and snacks for me, and because there was an immediate rapport between us (probably because this was the first time that she, the mother, could vent her frustrations), she invited me to lunch. The stories tumbled out from mother and daughter, and I felt both their conflicts and angst and their sense of pride and accomplishment.

The mother told me in detail that her daughter was a regular participant in dance contests and that she had won many gold medals due to her talent. The dance competitions on television provided a great opportunity for her daughter to display her talent in dance. She encouraged her daughter to participate in these reality show dance contests even though the demands by the choreographers were sometimes difficult. Once there were conflicts with a particular choreographer, she said, and both mother and daughter were unhappy about the choice of costumes for a reality show. Both of them talked about their embarrassment about this particular incident where the revealing costume that the daughter had worn snapped during the performance. To make the

---

[6] I am thinking about the chief minister of Bengal, Mamata Banerjee and her slogan of Ma, Mati, Manush (Mother, Land, Mankind), Human Resources Minister Smriti Irani (2014–16) posing as the Hindu Goddess Durga, and Jayalalithaa (the late chief minister of Tamil Nadu) as the self-appointed Amma/mother (a mutation of Ammu, her real name, to Amma, although she was childless).

matter worse, their family and friends viewed this event on live television. If they were mildly disapproving of her dancing before, this event shamed her and made her somewhat of an outcast. But still, the young woman said, she would not give up her dream of becoming a dancer and a choreographer. She would continue to compete in reality shows and the mother supported her completely. The mother confided in me that she was going against her husband's wishes and supporting her daughter.

Another contestant expressed similar sentiments regarding revealing and scanty costumes and a general disapproval by her university professors for choosing to be part of commercial television shows. During many of my interviews with the contestants and their mothers, I learned how the schools and colleges have been openly hostile towards these students, even going so far as to encourage other classmates to avoid their company. The sexual morality of the contestants of dance reality shows has been repeatedly scrutinized and questioned by academic authorities in public schools and colleges, and generally speaking, contestants and their families have been treated as corrupting influences on academic environments.

One mother confided to me that her daughter's independence in moving around because of her varying schedule (due to her rehearsals, auditions, and shootings) is what creates the environment of disapproval.[7] 'This is not so for girls who do regular jobs', observed the mother, adding: 'When my daughter is shown on reality shows the neighbors gossip that my daughter is coming back late at night because of such shows, and when my daughter is not on TV they suspiciously

[7] The policing of women's mobility has become a subject of intense debate in many cities after cases of rape, molestation, and 'eve teasing' filled the TV channels. The Nirbhaya case, when a 23-year-old female student was gang raped and murdered in a moving bus in Delhi, bolsters these debates.

ask where is your daughter, why is she not on this show?' She exclaimed in frustration that because they see her daughter on TV they think they can pass judgment. 'What is the right conduct for my daughter, since she will never get the approval of the general population?' One time a grandmother of a contestant told me vociferously that she would encourage her granddaughter to dance on reality shows as long as she was able, even if she was socially isolated for doing it. The time has come for women, she declared, to step out and claim a place in this changing world. She was clear that her granddaughter should have access to the avenues she needed to become successful, opportunities that had been denied to her when she was young.

In the context of this ongoing social transformation in India, Ruchira Ganguly-Scrase and Timothy Scrase (2009: 152) observe:

> The struggle to preserve middle-class culture and identity in the face of great social change highlights the way in which cultural politics is at the core of middle-class opposition to neoliberal reforms and, moreover, these cultural struggles take place as much within the relative privacy of the home, as in the public sphere of the street, the workplace or the tea shop. In other words, while neoliberal reforms have inexorably changed social and economic life, their indirect impact through globalised-induced cultural change has also been an affront to middle-class morals, culture, and identity.

The presentations of my research on dance reality shows at several conferences in India and the U.S. have also elicited such mixed responses from fellow academics and dancers and cultural pundits. I have received outright disapproval for my empathetic position regarding reality shows and their contestants; some in the audience have gone so far as to tell me that I am ignoring the exploitation of capitalism and the television industry. The contestants were just pawns and the dancing was immoral and vulgar. One person vehemently protested and said that my research was supporting the corruption of taste. People in the U.S. tended not to be bothered about the 'sexuality' or 'vulgarity' but many said that the shows did not reveal any artistic talent or creativity, and dismissed them as simply commercial entertainment, not art.[8]

Although these reactions partially represent a section of the middle classes, the narratives of the dancers and mothers I spoke to actively contest these sentiments and moral judgments. They clearly recognize the possibility of class mobility in the new economy—attitudes that were repeatedly apparent to me during my conversations not just with the contestants and their mothers, but with producers, recruiters, and choreographers. All of them routinely expressed the importance of platforms such as dance reality shows for providing opportunities to talented young adults who were not from well-connected or well-to-do families. Many contestants and their choreographers regularly pointed out that the platform had allowed them to launch their own dance or acting careers. Many from the small towns saw this as an opportunity to realize their dream of buying an apartment in Kolkata or a car. Often, winning a contest meant that the winner could buy an apartment like those displayed on billboards and hoardings all around them; in short, they could participate in the consumption practices of the middle-classes.

Many contestants and their parents articulated their ambivalence to the past codes of morality by explaining that those codes had denied them opportunities. Despite the fact that they did not blindly embrace the dictates of the market or uncritically celebrate commercial platforms like reality shows, they saw the shows as opening a crack in the

---

[8] These reactions marked the constructed nature of morality and art, especially to me, because my previous research on the tawaif and their stigmatization as prostitutes by respectable society during the turn of the twentieth century revealed similar judgments, albeit in a very different context. The desire to take the 'high moral ground' does not change, it seems, even if the context does.

door to participate in India's future—a door that had been fully shut for them in the past. At the same time, they repeatedly criticized the blatant commercialism and opportunism of reality shows. The manipulation of the audience and the winners by the television channels often left them frustrated and dejected. But their narratives revealed a fundamental irony of the market: that the same commercialism, opportunism, and manipulation of dance reality shows and Bollywood dance that were undoubtedly tied to the seductive world of celebrity culture, consumerism, media, and youth, had aided in a kind of gender and class liberation in India.

However, the idea of liberation remains moot. What kind of liberation is this when it is tied to the growing hegemony of Bollywood and its culture industry? Perhaps the answer lies in the new emotions of aspiration associated with 'remix'. As long as the experience remains fluid and non-codified (less a product and more an experience), the opportunity of freedom of movement accrues. Then 'remix' carries the potential of both improvisation and subversion. Above all, as long as the intimate moments of emotional transfer from the screen to the individual carries the spark to open up of one's own body to connect to another, the potential of change persists. This kind of liberation is not structural or tied to some political movement, but intimate and personal, tied to domestic and marginal spaces. Ultimately, this book shows that the significance of the most public of events such as dance reality shows, can be understood perhaps through the ethnographic eye on the most intimate spaces of individual desire and subjectivity.

Bibliography

Aaker, David. 1995. *Building Strong Brands*. New York: Free Press.

Abu-Lughod, Lila and Catherine A. Lutz. 1990. 'Introduction: Emotion, Discourse, and the Politics of Everyday Life.' In *Language and the Politics of Emotion*, Catherine A. Lutz and Lila Abu-Lughod (eds), pp. 1–23. Cambridge: Cambridge University Press.

Adorno, Theodor and Max Horkheimer. 1972. *The Dialectic of the Enlightenment*. New York: Herder and Herder.

Appadurai, Arjun and Carol Breckenridge. 1995. 'Public Modernity in India'. In *Consuming Modernity: Public Culture in a South Asian World*, Carol Breckenridge (ed.), pp. 1–20. Minneapolis: University of Minnesota Press.

Appadurai, Arjun. 1997. *Modernity at Large*. New Delhi: Oxford University Press.

Basu, Anustup. 2008. 'The Music of Intolerable Love: Political Conjugality and Dil Se'. In *Global Bollywood: Travels of Hindi Song and Dance*, Sangita Gopal and Sujata Moorti (eds), pp. 153–78. Minneapolis: University of Minnesota Press.

Bathing Babies in Three Cultures. 1954. Directed/Produced by Gregory Bateson and Margaret Mead. New York University Film Library.

Baudrillard, Jean. 1983. *Simulations*. (tr.) Paul Foss et al. New York: Semiotext (e).

Baviskar, Amita and Raka Ray (eds). 2011. *Elite and Everyman: The Cultural Politics of the Indian Middle Classes*. New Delhi: Routledge.

Bender, Shawn. 2005. 'Of Roots and Race: Discourses of Body and Place in Japanese Taliko Drumming'. *Social Science Japan Journal* 8(2): 197–212.

Benjamin, Walter. 1969. *Illuminations: Essays and Reflections*. Edited by Hannah Arendt, translated by Harry Zohn. New York: Chicken.

Berger, John. 1972. *Ways of Seeing: Based on the Television Series*. London: Penguin Books.

Berthas, Alain. 2000. *The Brain's Sense of Movement, Perspective in Cognitive Neuroscience*. Cambridge (MA): Harvard University Press.

Bhatti, Shaila and Christopher Pinney. 2011. 'Optic-Clash: Modes of Visuality'. In *A Companion to the Anthropology of India*. Edited by Isabelle Clark-Deces. London: Wiley Blackwell.

Behl, Aditya. 2012. *Love's Subtle Magic: An Indian Islamic Literary Tradition, 1379–1545*, (ed.) Wendy Doniger. New York: Oxford University Press.

Birdwhistell, Ray L. 1970. *Kinesics in Context: Essays on Body Motion Communication*. Philadelphia: University of Pennsylvania Press.

Blacking, John (ed.). 1977. 'Towards Anthropology of the Body'. In *The Anthropology of the Body*, pp. 1–28. London: Academic Press.

Booth, Gregory. 2000. 'Religion, Gossip, Narrative Conventions and the Construction of Meaning in Hindi Film Songs'. *Popular Music* 19: 125–46.

Born, Georgina. 2010. 'The Social and the Aesthetic: For a Post Bourdieuian Theory of Cultural Production'. *Cultural Sociology* 4(2): 171–208.

Bourdieu, Pierre. 1984. *Distinction: A Social Critique of the Judgement of Taste*, translated by Richard Nice. Cambridge, MA: Harvard University Press.

———. 1977. *Outline of a Theory of Practice, Cambridge Studies in Social and Cultural Anthropology*. Cambridge: Cambridge University Press.

Butler, Judith. 1999. *Subjects of Desire: Hegelian Reflections in 20th-Century France*. New York: Columbia University Press.

Carpenter, David. 2008. *Practice Makes Perfect: The Role of Practice Abhyasa in Patanjali Yoga in Yoga: The Indian Tradition* Ian Whicher and David Carpenter (ed.). London: Routledge.

Chakrabarty, Dipesh. 2000. *Provincializing Europe: Postcolonial Thought and Historical Differences*. Princeton, NJ: Princeton University Press.

Chakraborty, Kobita. 2015. *Young Muslim Women in India: Bollywood, Identity and Changing Youth Culture*. Routledge: London.

Chakravarty, Sumita S. 1993. *National Indian Identity in Indian Popular Cinema, 1947–87*. Austin: University of Texas Press.

Chakravorty, Pallabi. 2016. 'Sensory Screens, Digitized Desires: Dancing Rasa from Bombay Cinema to Reality TV'. In *The Oxford Handbook on Screen Dance Studies*, Douglas Rosenberg (ed.), pp. 125–42.

———. 2010. 'Global Dancing in Kolkata'. In *A Companion to the Anthropology of India*, Isabelle Clark-Deces (ed.), pp. 137–53. London: Wiley Blackwell.

———. 2009a. 'Moved to Dance: Remix, Rasa, and a New India'. *Visual Anthropology* 22(2–3): 211–28.

———. 2009b. 'The Exalted Body in North Indian Music and Dance'. In *Performing Ecstasy*, Pallabi Chakravorty and Scott Kugle (eds). New Delhi: Manohar Publishers.

———. 2008. *Bells of Change: Kathak Dance, Women, and Modernity in India*. Calcutta/Chicago: Seagull, University of Chicago Press.

———. 2007. 'Dancing into Modernity: The Multiple Narratives of India's Kathak Dance'. *Dance Research Journal* 38(1, 2): 115–36.

———. 2005. 'Bhakti in Modernity and Modernity in Bhakti: Kathak and Kabir'. *Moving Worlds: A Journal of Transcultural Writings* 5(2): 91–103.

———. 2004. 'Dance, Pleasure, and Indian Women as Multisensorial Subjects'. *Visual Anthropology* 17(1): 1–17.

———. 1998. 'Dance, Hegemony and Nation: The Construction of Classical Indian Dance'. *South Asia* XXI(2); 107–20.

Chatterjee, Gayatri. 2005. 'Icons and Events: Reinventing Visual Construction in Cinema in India'. In *Bollyworld: Popular Indian Cinema through a Transnational Lens*, Raminder Kaur and Ajay J. Sinha (eds), pp. 90–117. New Delhi: Sage.

Chatterjee, Partha. 1989. 'The Nationalist Resolution of the Women's Question'. In *Recasting Women: Essays in Colonial History*, Kumkum Sangari and Sudesh Vaid (eds), pp. 233–53. New Delhi: Kali for Women.

Child, Louise. 1998. *Tantric Buddhism and Altered States of Consciousness*. Burlington: Ashgate Publishing Limited.

Clifford, James and George E. Marcus (eds) 1986. *Writing Culture*. Berkley: University of California Press.

Coorlawala, Uttara A. 2004. 'The Sanskritized Body'. *Dance Research Journal* 36(2) Winter: 50–63.

Couglan, Sean. 2009. 'It's Hinglish, Innit?' February. *BBC News*. Available at: http://isites.harvard.edu/fs/docs/icb.topic543017.files/Contact%20and%20Convergence%20II/Required/Western%20Media%20on%20Hinglish/Its_Hinglish_innit.pdf (last accessed on 9 July 2017).

Crary, Jonathan. 1990. *Techniques of the Observer: On Vision and Modernity in the Nineteenth Century*. Cambridge: MIT Press.

Csordas, Thomas J. (ed.). 1994. *Embodiment and Experience: The Existential Ground of Culture and Self*. Cambridge: Cambridge University Press.

Cullity, J. 2002. 'The Global Desi: Cultural Nationalism on MTV India'. *Journal of Communication Inquiry* 26: 408–25.

Cynthia Jean Cohen (aka Cynthia Novack). 1997. 'Sense, Meaning, and Perception in Three Dance Cultures'. In *Meaning in Motion. New Cultural Studies of Dance*.

Dandayudapani, K. N. 1956. *Indian Talkie (1931–56)* (Silver Jubilee Souvenir). Bombay: Film Federation of India.

Dasgupta, Rohit and K. Moti Gokul Singh (eds). 2013. 'Introduction: Perceptions of Masculinity and Challenges to the Indian Male'. In *Masculinity and Its Challenges in India*, pp. 6–25. London: MacFarland.

Dasgupta, Sanjukta, Dipankar Sinha, and Sudeshna Chakrabarti (eds). 2011. *Media, Gender and Popular Culture in India*. New Delhi: Sage.

David, Ann R. 2010. 'Dancing the Diasporic Dream? Embodied Desires and the Changing Audiences for Bollywood Film Dance'. *Participations: Journal of Audience and Reception Studies* 7(2). Available at: http://www.participations.org/Volume%207/Issue%202/special/david.htm

David, Harvey. 1989. *The Condition of Postmodernity*. Oxford: Blackwell.

Deleuze, G. and F. Guattari. 1987. *A Thousand Plateaus: Capitalism and Schizophrenia*. Translated by B. Massumi. Minneapolis: University of Minnesota Press.

Deshpande, Sudhanva. 2005. 'The Consumable Hero of Globalized India'. In *Bollyworld: Popular Indian Cinema through a Transnational Lens*, Raminder Kaur and Ajay Sinha (eds), pp. 186–203. London: Sage.

Dimock, Edward C., Jr. 1989. *The Place of the Hidden Moon: Erotic Mysticism in the Vaisnava-sahajiya Cult of Bengal*. Chicago: University of Chicago Press.

Dodds, Sherill. 2005. *Dance on Screen: Genres and Media from Hollywood to Experimental Art*. London: Palgrave Macmillan.

Doniger, Wendy. 2011. *The Hindus: An Alternative History*. New York: Penguin.

Douglas, Mary. 1973. *Natural Symbols*. New York: Vintage.

Dudhra, Rajinder and Jigna Desai (eds). 2008. *The Bollywood Reader*. Berkshire: Open University Press.

Eck, Diana. 1998. *Darsan: Seeing the Divine Image in India*. Chambersburg: Anima Publications.

Ekman, Paul. 1977. 'Biological and Cultural Contributions to Body and Facial Movement'. In *The Anthropology of the Body*, John Blacking (ed.), pp. 34–84. London: Academic Press.

Farleigh, Sondra. 2000. 'Consciousness Matters'. *Dance Research Journal* 32(1): 54–62.

Farnell, Brenda. 2011. 'Theorizing "The Body" in Visual Culture'. In *Made to Be Seen: Perspectives on the History of Visual Anthropology*, Marcus Banks and Jay Ruby (eds), pp. 136–58. University of Chicago Press.

Fazal, Shehina. 2009. 'Emancipation or Anchored Individualism? Women and TV Soaps in India'. In *Popular Culture in a Globalized India*, K. Moti Gokulsing and Wimal Dissanayake (eds), pp. 41–52. New York: Routledge.

Fernandes, Leela. 2011. 'Hegemony and Inequality: Theoretical Reflections on India's "New" Middle Class'. In *Elite and Everyman*. Amita Baviskar and Raka Ray (eds), pp. 58–82. New Delhi: Routledge.

Finkelstein, Joanne. 1991. *The Fashioned Self*. Cambridge: Wiley Black-well.

Foster, Susan L. 2011. *Choreographing Empathy: Kinesthesia in Performance*. New York: Routledge.

Fox, Richard G. 1991. 'For a Nearly New Culture History'. In *Recapturing Anthropology: Working in the Present*, G. Fox (ed.), pp. 93–104. Santa Fe, New Mexico: School of American Research Press.

Ganguly-Scrase, Ruchira and Timothy J. Scrase. 2009. *Globalisation and the Middle Classes in India*. London: Routledge.

Ganti, Teja. 2012. *Producing Bollywood*. Durham: Duke University Press.

Geertz, Clifford. 1973. *The Interpretation of Culture: Selected Essays*. New York: Basic Books.

Gehlawat, Ajay. 2010. *Reframing Bollywood: Theories of Popular Hindi Cinema*. New Delhi: Sage.

Gopal, Sangita A. and Sujata Moorti (eds). 2008. *Global Bollywood: Travels of Hindi Song and Dance*. Minneapolis: University of Minnesota Press.

Gopalan, Lalitha. 2002. *Cinema of Interruptions: Action Genres in Contemporary Indian Cinema*. London: British Film Institute Publishing (Indian Reprint). Delhi: Oxford University Press.

Grossberg, Laurence. 1997. *Bringing It All Back Home*. Durham: Duke University Press.

Gupta, Nilanjana. 1998. *Switching Channels*. Delhi: Oxford University Press.

Gupta, Somenath. 2005. *The Parsi Theatre: Its Origins and Development*. Translated by Kathryn Hansen. Calcutta: Seagull Books.

Hall, Edward. 1968. 'Proxemics'. *Current Anthropology* 9(2–3): 83–108.

Hansen, Kathryn. 2003. 'The Indar Sabha Phenomenon: Public Theatre and Consumption in Greater India 1853–1956'. In *Pleasure and The Nation*, Rachel Dwyer and Christopher Pinney (eds), pp. 76–114. New Delhi; New York: Oxford University Press.

Haug, W.F. 1986. (Translated by Robert Bock). *Critique of Commodity Aesthetics: Appearance, Sexuality, and Advertising in Capitalist Society*. Minneapolis: University of Minnesota Press.

Hobsbawm, Eric and Terence Ranger (eds). 1983. *The Invention of Tradition*. Cambridge: Cambridge University Press.

Horkheimer, Max and Theodor W. Adorno. 1972. *The Dialectic of Enlightenment*. New York: Herder and Herder. Available at: http://archive.indianexpress.com/news/reality-strikes/335969/0, 2008, (last accessed on 9 July 2017).

Hymes, Dell. 1962. 'The Ethnography of Speaking'. In *Anthropology and Human Behavior*, T. Gladwin and W.C. Sturtevant (eds), pp. 13–53. Washington D.C.: Anthropological Society of Washington.

Iyer, Usha. 2014. *Film Dance, Female Stardom, and the Production of Gender in Popular Hindi Cinema*. University of Pittsburg, Ph.D. in English/Film Studies.

Jafri, H.N Sayed. 2010. 'Sufic Themes and Images in Persian and Hindavi Poetry'. *In Essays on Literature, History And Society*. New Delhi: Primus Books.

Jameson, Fredric. 1991. *Postmodernism, or The Cultural Logic of Late Capitalism.* Durham: Duke University Press.

Jameson, Fredric. 1998. 'Notes on Globalization as a Philosophical Issue'. In *The Cultures of Globalization,* Fredric Jameson and Masao Miyoshi (eds), pp. 54–77. Durham: Duke University Press.

Jhanji, Rekha. 2007. 'Rasanubhuti and Brahmananda: Some Parallels'. In *Approaches to Natya Shahtra,* Amrit Srinivasan (ed.), pp. 90–104. New Delhi: Centre for Studies in Civilizations for the Project of History of Indian Science, Philosophy and Culture and Matrix Pu.

Johnsen, Linda. 2014. *Tantra and the Teachings of Abhinava Gupta.* https://yogainternational.com/article/view/tantra-and-the-teachings-of-abhinavagupta.

Kaeppler, Adrienna. 1991. 'American Approaches to the Study of Dance'. In *Yearbook for Traditional Music,* D. Christensen (ed.), Geneva: International Council for Traditional Music.

Katrak, Ketu. 2011. *Contemporary Indian Dance: New Creative Choreography in India and the Diaspora.* New York: Palgrave Macmillan.

Kaur, Raminder and Ajay J. Sinha (eds). 2005. *Popular Indian Cinema through a Transnational Lens.* New Delhi: Sage Publications.

Kavka, Misha. 2008. *Reality Television, Affect, and Intimacy.* London (UK): Palgrave Macmillan.

Kedar, Anusha. 2014. 'Flexibility and Its Bodily Limits: Transnational South Asian Dancers in an Age of Neoliberalism'. *Dance Research Journal* 46(1): 23–40.

Kesavan, Mukul. 1994. 'Urdu, Awadh and the Tawaif: The Islamicate Roots of Hindi Cinema'. In *Forging Identities: Gender, Communities and the State,* Zoya Hasan (ed.), pp. 244–57. New Delhi: Kali for Women.

Khubchandani, Lata. 2004. *Encyclopedia of Hindi Cinema,* Govind Nihalani, Gulzar, and Saibal Chaterjee (eds). New Delhi: Popular Prakashan.

Knight, Douglas M. (Jr). *Balasaraswati: Her Art and Her Life.* Connecticut: Wesleyan University.

Kugle, Scott. 2007. '*Qawwālī* between Written Poem and Sung Lyric, or …How a *Ghazal* Lives'. *The Muslim World* 97(4): 571–610.

Kumar, Shanti. 2006. *Gandhi Meets Primetime: Globalization and Nationalism in Indian Television.* Illinois: University of Illinois Press.

Lacan, J. 1949/2010. 'The Mirror Stage'. In *Social Theory: The Multicultural, Global, and Classical Readings*, C. Lemert (ed.), pp. 343–44. Philadelphia: Westview Press.

Leavitt, John. 1996. 'Meaning and Feeling in the Anthropology of Emotions'. *American Ethnologist* 23(3): 514–39.

Leder, Drew. 1990. *The Absent Body*. Chicago: The University of Chicago Press.

Leenhardt, Maurice. 1979/1949. *Do Kamo: Person and Myth in Melanesian World*. Chicago: University of Chicago Press.

Levine, Robert A. 2007. 'Ethnographic Studies of Childhood: A Historical Overview'. *American Anthropologist* 109(2): 247–60.

Levinson, David and Melvin Ember (ed.). 1996. *Encyclopedia of Cultural Anthropology*. New York: Henry Holt and Company.

Malefyt, Timothy D. 2007. 'From Rational Calculation to Sensual Experience: The Marketing of Emotions in Advertising'. In *The Emotions: A Cultural Reader*, Helena Wulff (ed.).

Mankekar, Purnima. 2015. *Unsettling India: Affect, Temporality, and Transnationality*. Durham: Duke University Press.

———. 2004. 'Dangerous Desires: Television and Erotics in Late Twentieth Century India'. *Journal of Asian Studies* 63(2): 403–31.

———. 1999. *Screening Culture, Viewing Politics*. Durham: Duke University Press.

Marcus, George and Michael Fisher. 1986. *Anthropology as Cultural Critique: An Experimental Moment in the Human Sciences*. Chicago: University of Chicago Press.

Marglin, Frederique Apffel. 1985. *Wives of the God-King: Rituals of the Devadasis of Puri*. New Delhi: Oxford University Press.

Massumi, Brian. 2002. *Parables for the Virtual: Movement, Affect, Sensation*. Durham, NC: Duke University Press.

Mauss, Marcel. 1950. 'Les Techniques du Corps'. *Sociologie et Anthropologie*. Paris: Presses Universities de France.

———. 1934/1973. 'Techniques of the Body'. *Economy and Society* 2: 70–88.

Mazzarella, William. 2009. 'Affect: What Is It Good For?' In *Enchantment of Modernity: Empire, Nation, Globalization*, Saurabh Dubey (ed.), pp. 291–309. New Delhi: Routledge.

Mazzarella, William. 2004. 'Culture, Globalization, and Mediation'. *Annual Review of Anthropology* 33: 345–67.

———. 2003. *Shoveling Smoke: Advertising and Globalization in Contemporary India*. Durham, NC: Duke University Press.

McLuhan, Marshall. 1964/1994. *Understanding Media: The Extensions of Man*. Cambridge: MIT Press.

Meduri, Avanthi. 1988. 'Bharatnatyam—What Are You'? *Asian Theatre Journal* 5: 1–22.

Merleau-Ponty, Maurice. 1962. *Phenomenology of Perception*. (tr.) Colin Smith. London: Routledge.

Mishra, Abhimanyu. 2011. *Hottest Bollywood Itemboys of 2011*. Available at: http://timesofindia.indiatimes.com/entertainment/hindi/bollywood/news/Hottest-Bollywood-item-boys-of-2011/articleshow/11306047.cms (last accessed on 9 July 2017).

Mishra, Vijay. 2002. *Bollywood Cinema: Temples of Desire*. New York: Routledge.

Mitra, Royona. 2015. *Akram Khan: Dancing New Interculturalism*. London: Palgrave.

Morelli, Sarah. 2010. Intergenerational Adaptation in North Indian Kathak Dance. *Anthropological Notebooks* 16(3): 77–91.

Morcom, Anna. 2013. *Illicit Worlds of Indian Dance: Cultures of Exclusion*. New York: Oxford University Press.

Mules, Warwick. 2007. 'Aura as Productive Loss'. *Transformations* (5), available at: http://www.transformationsjournal.org/issues/15/article_05.shtml (last accessed on 9 July 2017).

Mulvey, Laura. 1975. 'Visual Pleasure and Narrative Cinema'. *Screen* 16(3) (Autumn): 6–18.

Munsi, Urmimala Sarkar. 2011. 'Imag(in)ing the Nation: Uday Shankar's Kalpana'. In *Traversing Tradition: Celebrating Dance in India*, Stephanie Burridge and Urmimala Sarkar Munsi (eds), pp. 124–50. New Delhi: Routledge.

Nandy, Asish. 1998. *The Secret Politics of Our Desire*. London: Zed Books.

Ness, Sally Ann. 1995. 'When Seeing Is Believing: The Changing Role of Visuality in a Philippine Dance'. *Anthropological Quarterly* 68(1) (January): 1–13.

———. 1992. *Body, Movement, and Culture*. Philadelphia: University of Pennsylvania Press.

Nihalani, Govind, Gulzar, and Saibal Chaterjee. (eds). 2004. *Encyclopaedia of Hindi Cinema*. Delhi: Popular Prakashan.

Ninan, Sevanti. 2000. 'History of Indian Broadcasting Reform'. In *Broadcasting Reform in India*, Monroe E. Price and Stefaan G. Verhulst (eds), pp. 1–22. New Delhi: Oxford University Press.

Novack, David. 2010. 'Cosmopolitanism, Remediation and the Ghost World of Bollywood'. *Cultural Anthropology* 25(1): 40–72.

Osumare, Halifu. 2002. 'Break Dancing and the Intercultural Body'. *Dance Research Journal* 34(2): 30–45.

Pandian, Anand. 2015. *An Anthropology of Creation*. Durham: Duke University Press.

Patel, Baburao. 1948. *Filmindia*. October.

Pathak, Gauri. 2014. '"Presentable": The Body and Neoliberal Subjecthood in Contemporary India'. *Social Identities* 20(4–5): 314–29.

Pinney, Christopher. 2002. 'The Indian Work of Art in the Age of Mechanical Reproduction: Or What Happens When Peasants "Get Hold" of Images'. In *Media Worlds: Anthropology on a New Terrain*, F.D Ginsburg, L. Abu-Lughod, and B. Larkin (eds), pp. 355–69. Berkeley: University of California Press.

———. 1997. 'The Nation (Un)Pictured: Chromolithography and Popular Politics in India, 1878–1995'. In 'Frontlines and Borderposts', special issue of *Critical Inquiry*, Homi Bhabha (ed.), 23(4) (Summer): 834–67.

Plantinga, Carl. 2009. *Moving Viewers*. Berkeley: University of California Press.

Plantinga, Carl and Greg M. Smith (eds). 1999. *Passionate. Views: Film, Cognition, and Emotion*. Baltimore and London: The Johns Hopkins.

Postman Neil. 1985. *Amusing Ourselves to Death: Public Discourse in the Age of Show Business*. London: Penguin.

Prasad, Madhav. 1998. *The Ideology of Hindi Films*. New Delhi: Oxford University Press.

Punathambekar, Aswin and Anandam P. Kavoori (eds). 2008. *Global Bollywood*. New York University Press.

Purkayastha, Prarthana. 2014. *Indian Modern Dance, Feminism and Transnationalis*. London: Palgrave Macmillan.

Raha, Shuma. 2008. 'Young Hearts Break the Best'. *The Telegraph*. Available at http://www.telegraphindia.com/1080710/jsp/opinion/story_9525697.jsp.

Raheja, Dinesh. 'Guide: A Human Odyssey'. Available at http://www.rediff. com/entertai/2002/apr/18dinesh.htm.

Rajadhyaksha, Asish. 2008. 'The Bollywoodization of the Indian Cinema: Cultural Nationalism in a Global Arena'. In *Global Bollywood*, Aswin Punathambekar and Anandam P. Kavoori (eds), pp. 17–40. New York: University Press.

Ramanathan, Sharada. 2010. 'A Cultural Affirmation'. *The Hindu*. thehindu. com/opinion/oped/article939951.ece?homepage=true), (last accessed on 10 December 2015).

Ramanujan, A.K. 1989. 'Is There an Indian Way of Thinking? An Informal Essay'. *Contributions to Indian Sociology* 23(41).

Rao, K.R. 2011. *Cognitive Anomalies, Consciousness, and Yoga*. New Delhi, Sangeet Natak Akademy.

Rosaldo, Michelle Zimbalist. 1980. *Knowledge and Passion: Ilongot Notions of Self and Social Life*. Cambridge: Cambridge University Press.

Roy, Anjali G. 2010. 'Is Everybody Saying "Shava Shava" to Bollywood Bhangra'. In *Bollywood and Globalization: Indian Popular Cinema, Nation, and Diaspora*, Rini Bhattacharya Mehta and Rejeshwari V. Pandharipande (eds). New York: AnthemPress.

Roy, Abhijit. 2014. 'TV after Television Studies: Recasting Questions of Audiovisual Form'. In *Channeling Cultures: Television Studies from India*, B. Sen and A Roy (eds). New Delhi: Oxford University Press.

Ruby, Jay. 1980. 'Franz Boas and Early Camera Study of Human Behavior'. *Kinesics Report*, (1–16). [www.temple.eduIanthro/ruby/boas/html].

Ruby, Jay. 1996. 'Anthropology'. In *Encyclopedia of Cultural Anthropology*, David Levinson and Melvin Ember (eds), pp. 1345–51 (vol. 4). New York: Henry Holt and Company.

Ruby, Jay. 1980. 'Exposing Yourself: Reflexivity, Anthropology, and Film'. *Semiotica* 30(1–2): 153–79.

Rustomji, Roshni. 1981. '"Rasa" and "Dhvani" in Indian and Western Poetics and Poetry'. *Journal of South Asian Literature* 16.1(Winter, Spring): 75–91, East West Literary Relations.

Salih, Sarah. 2002. *Judith Butler (Routledge Critical Thinkers)*. London: Routledge.

Schechner, Richard. 2001. 'Rasaesthetics'. *The Drama Review* 45(3): 27–50.

Schwartz, Susan L. 2004. 'Rasa: Performing the Divine in India. Locana, 2.4'. In Ingalls, Nasson, and Patwardhan (eds), p. 17. New York: Columbia University Press.

Sen, Biswarup. 2014. 'Big Brother Big Boss'. In *Channeling Cultures: Television Studies from India*, B. Sen and A Roy (eds). New Delhi: Oxford University Press.

———. 2008. 'The Sounds of Modernity: The Evolution of Bollywood Film Song'. In *Global Bollywood: Travels of Hindi Song and Dance*, Sangita Gopal and Sujata Moorti (eds), pp. 85–104. Minneapolis: University of Minnesota Press.

Sengupta, Shuddhabrata. 2005. 'Reflected Readings in Available Light: Cameramen in the Shadows of Hindi Cinema.' In *Popular Indian Cinema through a Transnational Lens*, Raminder Kaur and Ajay J. Sinha (eds), pp. 118–40. New Delhi: Sage.

Shaviro, Steven. 1993. *The Cinematic Body (Theory Out of Bounds)*. Minneapolis: University of Minnesota Press.

Sheth, D. L. 1999. 'Secularization of Caste and Making of New Middle Class'. *Economic and Political Weekly* 34(34/35): 2502–10.

Shresthova, Sangita. 2011. *Is It All About Hips?* New Delhi: Sage Publications.

———. 2003. 'Strictly Bollywood? Story, Camera, and Movement in Hindi Film Dance' (Master's thesis, MIT).

Silverman, Hugh J. (ed.) 2006. *Philosophy and Desire*. New York: Routledge.

Silverman, Kaja. 1996. *The Threshold of the Visible*. New York: Routledge.

Sinha, Mrinalini. 2014. 'Gendered Nationalism'. In *Routledge Handbook of Gender in South Asia*, Leela Fernandes (ed.), pp. 13–27. New Delhi: Routledge.

Smith, Paul. 2008. *The Ghazal in Sufi and Dervish Peotry* (Translations and Introduction). Victoria: New Humanity Books.

Sol Worth, William. 1981. *Studying Visual Communication*, (ed.) Larry Gross. Philadelphia: University of Pennsylvania.

Soneji, Davesh. 2012. *Unfinished Gestures: Devadasis, Memory, and Modernity in South India*. Chicago: University of Chicago Press.

Srinivasan, Priya. 2012. *Sweating Saris: Indian Dance as Transnational Labor*. Philadelphia: Temple University.

Stoller, Paul. 1997. *Sensuous Scholarship*. Philadelphia: University of Pennsylvania Press.

———. 1989. *The Taste of Ethnographic Things: The Senses in Anthropology.* Philadelphia: University of Pennsylvania.

Stratton, Jon. 1996. *The Desirable Body: Cultural Fetishism and the Erotics of Consumption.* Manchester: Manchester University Press.

Sumi, Sukanya. 2015. 'Centre Targets 'Cultural Pollution''. *The Telegraph.* http://www.telegraphindia.com/1150908/jsp/frontpage/story_41407.jsp#.VfMfyla2PFI.

Sundar, Pavithra. 2014. 'Of Radio, Remix, and Rang De Basanti: Rethinking History through Film Sound'. *Jump Cut: A Review of Contemporary Media* 56 (Fall). (http://www.ejumpcut.org/currentissue/RangDeBasanti/text.html cessed), (accessed 31 July 2015).

Tagore, Rabindranath. 1930. *The Religion of Man.* Oxford: Manchester College.

Taussig, Michael. 1992. *The Nervous System.* New York: Routledge.

Taylor, Woodman. 2002. 'Penetrating Gazes: The Poetics of Sight and Visual Display in Popular Indian Cinema'. *Contributions to Indian Sociology* 36: 297–322.

The Indian Express. 2011. 'Is It sunset for Bollywood's Magnificent "sets"?' July 17 (last accessed in January 2012).

Thomas, Rosie. 2005. 'Not Quite (Pearl): Fearless Nadia, Queen of the Stunts.' In *Bollywood: Popular India Cinema through a Transnational Lens*, R. Kaur and A.J. Jain (eds), pp. 35–69. New Delhi: Sage.

Thussu, Daya Kishan. 2013. *Communicating India's Soft Power: Buddha to Bollywood.* New York: Palgrave Macmillan.

———. 2008. 'The Globalization of "Bollywood": The Hype and Hope'. In *Global Bollywood*, Aswin Punathambekar and Anandam P. Kavoori (eds), pp. 17–40. New York University Press.

Trance and Dance in Bali. 1951. Directed/Produced by Margaret Mead and Gregory Bateson. New York University Film Library.

Trivia Time# 33. http://memsaabstory.com/2008/12/14/trivia-time-33/.

Vasudevan, Ravi (ed.). 2000. *Making Meaning in Indian Cinema.* New Delhi: Oxford University Press.

Vatsyayan, Kapila. 1977. *Classical Indian Dance in Literature and the Arts.* New Delhi: Sangeet Natak Akademi.

Vishnu, A. 2003. 'Age of "Hinglish" Remixes'. *The Hindu*. August 2003 (accessed 3 August 2011).

Walker, Margaret. 2014. *India's Kathak Dance in Historical Perspective*. Surrey: Ashgate Publishing Limited.

Wegenstein, Bernadette and Nora Ruck. 2011. 'Physiognomy, Reality Television, and the Cosmetic Gaze'. *Body and Society* 27(17): 27–55.

Weidman, Amanda. 2012. 'Voices of Meenakumari: Sound, Meaning, and Self-Fashioning in Performances of an Item Number'. *Journal of South Asian Popular Culture* 10(3) (July): 307–18.

Williams, Drid. 1991. *Ten Lectures on Theories of Dance*. London: Scarecrow Press.

Williams, Raymond. 1974. *Television, Technology, and Cultural Form*. New York: Routledge.

Wolputte, Steven Van. 2004. 'Hang On to Yourself: Of Bodies, Embodiment, and Selves'. *Annual Review of Anthropology* 33: 251–69.

Worth, Sol. 1976. 'Doing the Anthropology of Visual Communication'. In Doing the Anthropology of Visual Communication. Working Papers in Culture and Communication 1(2): 2–20.

Zylinksa, Joanna. 2009. *Bioethics in the Age of New Media*. Cambridge: The MIT Press.

Zelinsky, Siegfried. 2006. *Deep Time of the Media: Towards an Archaeology of Hearing and Seeing by Technical Means*. Cambridge: MIT Press.

Zizek, Slavoj. 1997. *The Plague of Fantasies*. New York: Verso.

Online Sources

http://www.indiaforums.com/celebrity/9936/remo-dsouza/biography/ (last accessed in May 2012).

http://www.mughaleazam.in, last accessed on 19 May 2015.

http://www.thehindu.com/thehindu/mp/2003/08/06/stories/2003080600090300/

http://indianexpress.com/article/entertainment/television/dance-shows-ontv-changed-bollywoods-dancing-style-remo-dsouza/

https://en.wikipedia.org/wiki/Mughal-e-Azam.50thanniversary.

Index

About the Author

Pallabi Chakravorty is Director of Dance and Associate Professor in the Department of Music and Dance at Swarthmore College, USA. Her ethnographic research in India has resulted in several publications spread through journals of dance, anthropology, history, and literary studies and her choreographies. Her book *Bells of Change: Kathak Dance, Women and Modernity in India* (Seagull/University of Chicago, 2008) is the first critical history and in-depth ethnographic account of Kathak dance and its practitioners. She has co-edited two books (*Performing Ecstasy: The Poetics and Politics of Religion in India*, 2009, and *Dance Matters: Performing India on Local and Global Stages*, 2010) and has edited the proceedings of an international symposium titled 'Dance in South Asia: New Approaches, Politics, and Aesthetics' (Swarthmore College, USA, 2002). She is currently co-editing another book: *Dance Matters Too*. She is the founder and artistic director of Courtyard Dancers, a non-profit dance company based in Philadelphia and Kolkata (www.courtyarddancers.org).